Peter of Ailly
and the Harvest of
Fourteenth-Century Philosophy

Leonard A. Kennedy

Studies in the History of Philosophy
Volume Two

The Edwin Mellen Press
Queenston/Lewiston

Library of Congress Cataloging-in-Publication Data

Kennedy, Leonard A.
 Peter of Ailly and the harvest of fourteenth-century
philosophy.

   (Studies in the history of philosophy ; v. 2)
   Bibliography: p.
   Includes index.
   1. Ailly, Pierre d', 1350-1420? I. Title.
II. Series: Studies in the history of philosophy
(Lewiston, N.Y.) ; v. 2.
B765.A34K46 1986   189'.4   86-23527
ISBN 0-88946-307-7

This is volume 2 in the continuing series
Studies in the History of Philosophy
Volume 2 ISBN 0-88946-307-7
SHP Series ISBN 0-88946-300-X

The Edwin Mellen Press   The Edwin Mellen Press
Box 450   Box 67
Lewiston, New York   Queenston, Ontario
USA 14092   CANADA LOS 1LO

Printed in the United States of America

To My
MOTHER
and to
KATHLEEN
and
BARBARA
My Sisters

STUDIES IN THE HISTORY OF PHILOSOPHY

CONTENTS

INTRODUCTION

More has been known about philosophy in the thirteenth century than in the fourteenth. Much recent research has been addressed to righting this imbalance. The introduction of new Greek, Arabic, and Hebrew materials in the early thirteenth century produced an intellectual ferment resulting, about 1270, in the Augustinian, Averroistic, and Thomistic philosophical systems. These were to continue to exist but, by the early fourteenth century, Scotism and Ockhamism were to become powerful rivals. By far the most influential school was the last-named, Ockhamism or Nominalism; this is becoming ever more evident to researchers. It is also becoming evident that, though, as has been pointed out [4, v. 39, p. 231], William of Ockham himself (c.1285 - 1347) was not nearly as sceptical as many of his followers, his doctrine contained the seeds that were to yield a harvest of scepticism [13; 25; 32].

This scepticism was philosophical, not theological. Though we might wonder how it could have been possible, the sceptics of the fourteenth century seem to have believed in Christian revelation. Indeed, one of the chief causes of philosophical scepticism involved belief in a revealed doctrine: the omnipotence of God. It was a particular interpretation of this doctrine that helped to diminish the trust of human reason in its ability to arrive at truth. What we shall do in this present work is show how Peter of Ailly's interpretation of divine omnipotence removes

1

necessity from the natural order and the supernatural order and leaves the human mind with assurance of very, very little concerning either the created universe or the Creator. It is true that many persons in the few decades before him had a similar interpretation and drew similar consequences, the best known of these being Nicholas of Autrecourt [18]; but Peter was to outdo them all in the extent and thoroughness of his project.

Peter was born in Compiègne, north of Paris, about 1350. He entered the University of Paris with a scholarship at the College of Navarre, and obtained his B.A. degree in 1367. He taught in the Faculty of Arts and then entered the Faculty of Theology. He was Bachelor of the Bible 1374-76, Bachelor of the Sentences 1376-77, and a Formed Bachelor 1377-81, receiving his Doctorate in Theology in 1381. He was named Canon of the Cathedral Chapter in Noyon in 1381, was Rector of the College of Navarre 1383-84, and Chancellor of the University of Paris 1389-95. Having been made Chaplain and Confessor to King Charles VI in 1389, he was named Archdeacon of Cambrai in 1391, Bishop of LePuy in 1395, Bishop of Cambrai in 1397, and Cardinal in 1411.

Peter's philosophical work gave way early in his career to administrative duties and to important ecclesiastical writings and negotiations concerning schism in the Church. He played a dominant role at the Council of Constance (1414-18) and died at Avignon in 1420.

He was an indefatigable worker. Tschackert
and Salembier have listed more than 170 writings by
him, and Glorieux has recently updated the list and the
dates of the works [60; 55; 15]. A great many of these
works deal with the government of the Church, abuses in
the church, the ending of schism, and the holding of a
General Council. Some are on scripture or on dogmatic,
moral, or ascetical questions. Some concern logic,
geography, astronomy, or astrology. Some are sermons
or hymns. The chief work relating to our topic,
however, is Peter's Commentary on the Sentences of
Peter Lombard.

Though Peter died long before the invention
of printing, most of his writings found their way into
print. His Commentary, composed 1376-77, went through
seven editions by the end of the fifteenth century. It
was published in Brussels in 1478, in Strassburg in
1490, in Paris in 1499, and again in Paris, probably in
1499. In 1500 it was printed in Lyons, in Venice, and
in an unidentified place. Peter's Tractatus de anima,
written about 1372, was published in Paris in 1494 and
again in 1505.

In the Commentary, the persons Peter mentions
most frequently are Aristotle, St. Augustine, William
of Ockham, Gregory of Rimini, and Adam Wodeham.
Authors mentioned much less frequently include
Boethius, St. John Damascene, Avicenna, Richard of St.
Victor, Robert Grosseteste, St. Thomas Aquinas, Duns
Scotus, Peter Aureol, John of Ripa, Robert Holkot,
Richard Fitzralph, Thomas Buckingham, and Hugolino of

3

Orvieto. Peter also mentions his fellow commentators on the _Sentences_, and Glorieux has tried to identify these [14, p. 63]. Besides his frequent references to Ockham, two manuscripts of Peter's give evidence that he was greatly influenced by Ockham. A large one (414 pp.) in the library of Anvers is a table of the contents of Ockham's works, and a smaller one (176 pp.) in the Bibliothèque Nationale is an abridgement of dialogues of Ockham [54, col. 1154-55].

At the end of this study of Peter is a selective bibliography. A complete one would be too lengthy, but it could be compiled from the sources listed here. For the sake of brevity, when reference is made to works in the bibliography, only the number of the work and the relevant pages will be cited. In the case of references to Peter's _Commentary_, only S (for _Sentences_), the book, and article, and alphabetical subdivision, will be given. These are sufficient since the only edition of the work readily available is the Minerva (Frankfurt, 1968) reprint of the Strassburg (1490) edition, which carries these alphabetical subdivisions. It has been noticed also that the Lyons edition carries the same divisions. Unfortunately the only other edition available to me (Lyons, 1500) contains all the mistakes of the Strassburg edition, so that the corrections I have occasionally made could not be checked by using another editions. I have also made some improvements in the punctuation of the texts cited, and capitalized a few words such as _Deus_ or _Spiritus Sanctus_ or _Sortes_. When corrections have been made in a reading, the incorrect

reading is also indicated. Please also note that,
since so many texts are cited in translation throughout
this work, the even-numbered pages from here until the
Bibliography have been reserved exclusively for the
Latin text of these quotations.

. . . duplex est evidentia. Quedam est evidentia absoluta qualis est evidentia primi principii vel reducibilis ad eam. Alia est evidentia condicionata qualis est evidentia nostri ingenii que est citra primam [S I 1 E].

. . . nulla evidentia condicionata . . . est infallibilis . . . [S I 1 O].

CERTAINTY

A sceptic is a person who denies the ability of the human mind to obtain certainty. Since this denial admits of degrees, a sceptic is one who limits the mind's ability to what others consider an excessive extent. Let us see how much Peter limits the mind's ability to obtain certainty.

According to Peter, there are two kinds of evidence. Absolute evidence is that given by the first principle (the principle of contradiction) or what can be reduced to it. All other evidence is conditional and fallible.

> There are two kinds of evidence. One is absolute evidence such as the evidence of the first principle or of what is reducible to it. The other is conditional evidence such as the evidence our mind has other than the first kind.

No conditional evidence is infallible.

Peter uses evidence as synonymous with assent, a use strange to modern ears, for which assent

. . . omnis evidentia est assensus licet non
econtra [S I 1 E].

Evidentia absoluta simpliciter potest
describi quod est assensus verus sine
formidine, causatus naturaliter, quo non est
possibile intellectum assentire et in sic
assentiendo decipi vel errare [S I 1 E].

Evidentia autem secundum quid potest describi
quod est assensus verus sine formidine,
causatus naturaliter, quo non est possibile,
stante Dei influentia generali et nullo facto
miraculo, intellectum assentire et in sic
assentiendo decipi vel errare [S I 1 E].

8

is a _reaction_ to evidence. Evidence, of course, is not
any kind of assent, but only true assent, and firm
assent, without fear of error. Moreover, it is caused
naturally. And it rules out the possibility of
deception or error. Absolute evidence rules out this
possibility necessarily, but conditional evidence does
so only if God is not interfering miraculously in the
ordinary state of affairs.

All evidence is assent, though not vice
versa.

Evidence which is simply absolute can be
described as an assent which is true, without
fear [of error], caused naturally, and such
that it is not possible for the intellect to
assent to it and in thus assenting be
deceived or err.

Conditional evidence, however, can be
described as assent which is true, without
fear [of error], caused naturally, and such
that it is not possible for the intellect to
assent to it and in thus assenting be
deceived or err provided God's general
influence is at work and no miracle has been
performed.

9

. . . causatus naturaliter, id est ex causis necessitantibus intellectum ad sic assentiendum, ad differentiam fidei que, licet sit assensus sine formidine, tamen non causatus naturaliter sed libere . . . [S I 1 E].

. . . possibile est viatoren non solum de primo principio sed etiam de multis aliis veritatibus habere evidentiam absolutam sive noticiam simpliciter evidentem [S I 1 E].

. . . quia quilibet experitur non solum primum principium esse sibi evidens modo predicto sed etiam multas consequentias, sicut . . . : si equus currit, animal currit, etc. [S I 1 E].

Evidence is said to be naturally caused in order to distinguish it from faith in divine revelation. Evidence is necessitated; faith, on the other hand, is a free assent, though it too is made without fear of error.

> Caused naturally, that is, by causes necessitating the intellect to assent in this way. This is unlike faith, which is not caused naturally but freely, though it is an assent without fear [of error].

It would seem that the human mind cannot know very much with absolute evidence, or knowledge simply speaking, though Peter initially states otherwise.

> It is possible for the wayfarer to have absolute evidence, or simply evident knowledge, not only concerning the first principle but also concerning many other truths.

It can know any conclusions following necessarily from the first principle, such as that, if a horse is running, and a horse is an animal, an animal is running.

> Because everyone experiences not only that the first principle is evident to him in the aforesaid manner but also many consequences, such as: if a horse is running, an animal is running, etc.

. . . quia aliter sequitur omnes scientias
perire, quod est inconveniens, maxime de
mathematicis quae secundum philosophum sunt
in primo gradu certitudinis [S I 1 E].

. . . possibile est viatorem de multis
veritatibus contingentibus habere evidentiam
absolutam . . . , verbi gratia quod ipse est,
quod ipse cognoscit, etc. Probatur per
Augustinum, XV de Trinitate, capitulo xii [S
I 1 E].

. . . aliqua humana noticia de aliquo
contingenti vero est infallibilis, puta
noticia qua scio me esse, vivere. Patet quia
non potest esse noticia et quod aliter sit
quam significat . . . [S I 1 O].

Sciences such as mathematics also yield absolute
evidence. But we shall see that for Peter there
probably are no sciences in the same class as
mathematics.

Because otherwise it follows that all the
sciences perish. This is unacceptable,
especially as regards mathematics which,
according to the Philosopher, is in the first
degree of certitude.

Similarly some contingent truths can be known with
absolute evidence. A person can know that he exists,
and that he knows, and so on, as St. Augustine said.

It is possible for the wayfarer to have
absolute evidence concerning many contingent
truths. For example, that he exists, that he
knows, etc. This is proved through
Augustine, On the Trinity, XV, Chapter 12.

Some human knowledge concerning some
contingent truth is infallible, such as the
knowledge by which I know that I exist, that
I live. This is evident because there cannot
be knowledge and yet things be other than as
it signifies.

Imo in evidentia sunt gradus. Quia primum
principium est evidentissimum. Et deinde
alia magis vel minus, secundum quod magis vel
minus appropinquant ad primum principium [S I
1 K].

. . . intellectus potest primo principio
dissentire quia Deus posset huiusmodi
dissensum in eo causare, de sua omnipotentia,
cum hoc non implicet contradictionem [S I 1
G].

Absolute evidence admits of degrees. The first principle is most evident, and other objects more or less evident as they are closer to or farther away from it, though all these are absolutely evident.

> Indeed, there are degrees in evidence because the first principle is most evident and then other things more or less evident according as they are more or less close to the first principle.

It is clear then that all absolute evidence depends on the first principle. Without it, all absolute evidence goes. Yet Peter is willing to raise the question whether a person can dissent from the first principle, and we will see Peter finally admit that one can. The suggestion is that God, being omnipotent, could cause this. God, of course, cannot do what is contradictory, but why, Peter thinks, would this be contradictory?

> The intellect can dissent from the first principle because God can cause this kind of dissent in it by His omnipotence, since this does not imply a contradiction.

Peter agrees that such a possibility is not opposed to the Christian faith (no doubt he is thinking of scriptural texts). Moreover, it seems to favour the doctrine of God's omnipotence because it exalts the divine power so much.

. . . dicere quod Deus possit huiusmodi assensum vel dissensum causare non contradicit fidei. Imo videtur favere articulo de omnipotentia Dei [S I 1 H].

. . . huiusmodi positio non est contraria veritati primi principii, et ad hanc positionem non sequitur "aliquis assentit opposito primi principii; ergo primum principium est falsum" [S I 1 H].

. . . quod Deus non posset se solo causare errorem [the text adds rem] de primo principio [S I 1 J].

To say that God can cause an assent or a dissent of this kind does not contradict faith. Indeed, it seems to favor the article [of faith] concerning the omnipotence of God.

It is not a question of God making the first principle false, but of God making someone <u>think</u> it is false. It would not be a contradiction for this to happen because the contradictory of "a person thinks the first principle is false" is "a person does not think the first principle is false," not "the first principle is false." Now, if it is not a contradiction, God can bring it about.

A position of this kind is not contrary to the truth of the first principle, and "someone assents to the opposite of the first principle; therefore the first principle is false" does not follow from this position.

God, however, cannot cause this error by Himself, since He does not directly cause evil.

Because God could not by Himself cause an error concerning the first principle.

Moreover, God cannot cause it in the ordinary course of things either, because in the ordinary course of things it would have to be caused as a by-product of knowing

. . . quod Deus, mediantibus causis secundis
iuxta naturam iam eis inditam de cursu
solito, non potest causare errorem de primo
principio, id est dissensum eius vel assensum
de eius opposito. Patet quia hoc esset ex
cognitione alicuius rei, sed quelibet
cognitio nata est concausare assensum primi
principii; saltem nulla est nata concausare
dissensum, plus quam caliditas nata est
frigefacere vel econtra [S I 1 J].

. . . Deus mediantibus causis secundis et de
suo posse absoluto potest causare errorem de
primo principio. Quia hoc non implicat, nec
hoc infert, contraria esse in eodem [S I 1
J].

something else, but all knowledge naturally causes at the same time an assent to the first principle; at least it cannot cause dissent from it, any more than heat of its nature can cause coldness.

Because God, through the mediation of secondary causes acting according to the nature already placed in them according to the ordinary course [of nature], cannot cause an error concerning the first principle, that is, dissent from it, or assent to its opposite. This is evident because this would be through a knowledge of something, but any knowledge naturally causes at the same time an assent to the first principle. At least no knowledge naturally causes at the same time dissent [from the first principle], any more than heat naturally cools, or vice versa.

Thus, since God can cause an intellect to dissent from the first principle, but cannot do it by Himself or by His ordinary power, He does it through the intermediary of secondary causes, and by His absolute power.

Through the mediation of secondary causes, and by His absolute power, God can cause an error concerning the first principle, because this does not imply, or lead to the conclusion, that contraries exist in the same subject.

. . . videtur mihi probabile . . . quod
intellectus, ex imperio voluntatis et prava
affectione cum aliqua apparentia licet falsa,
posset naturaliter dissentire primo principio
[S I 1 J].

Deus potest facere aliquem intellectum tante
perfectionis et talis conditionis quod ex
sola determinatione voluntatis sufficiet
assentire quibuscumque veris sibi propositis
. . . quia non apparet quod talem intellectum
a deo fieri implicet contradictionem [S I
principium R; see the same words in S I
principium G].

As for the secondary causes, these would probably be human wills which, affected by a false appearance, can order their intellects to dissent from the first principle.

> It seems to me probable that the intellect, from the command of the will, and affected in a disordered manner by an appearance which is false, can naturally dissent from the first principle.

In other texts Peter is not worried about God's causing this by intermediaries. He simply states that God can make an intellect such that it accepts as true whatever its will proposes to it as true. God can do this because it doesn't seem to imply a contradiction.

> God can make an intellect of such perfection and of such a condition that, from the determination of the will alone, it will be capable of assenting to any truths proposed to it, because it does not seem that such an intellect being made by God implies a contradiction.

As for God's absolute power, Peter makes great use of this notion. God's absolute power was contrasted with His ordained power. Unfortunately these powers were defined in different ways at different times, or by different authors at the same time, and were sometimes used without being defined.

Sed Deum aliquid posse de potentia ordinata
potest dupliciter intelligi. Uno modo
stricte quod potest stante sua ordinatione
qua eternaliter voluit se sic vel sic esse
facturum . . . . Alio modo potest intelligi,
magis large, quod potest stante veritate
legis ordinate seu scripture divine [S I 13
D].

. . . sed illud dicitur posse de potentia
absoluta quod absolute et simpliciter potest
quamvis oppositum ordinaverit vel revelaverit
[S I 13 D].

Courtenay has traced the history of these definitions [7]. For our purposes we can use the definition given by Peter of Ailly. For Peter, we can understand God's ordained power in two senses. In the stricter sense, it is the power used by God in the physical, moral, or supernatural orders which He has established or which He will establish in the future; that is, the power He has eternally decreed He will use. In the wider sense, it is any power God can use which is not incompatible with what He has revealed.

> But "God being able to do something by His ordained power" can be understood in two ways. In one way, speaking strictly: what He can do within His decree by which He eternally willed that He would act in such and such a way. In another way it can be understood more broadly: what He can do without violating the law He has established, or divine scripture.

We shall henceforth understand God's ordained power in this wider sense.

> For Peter, God has power to do things incompatible with what He has ordained or revealed. This power is His absolute power.

> But He is said to be able to do by His absolute power what He can do absolutely and simply, even though He has decreed or revealed the opposite.

23

Deus dicitur omnipotens quia potest facere
omne factibile, sive omne illud quod fieri
non implicat contradictionem [S I 13 A].

. . . Deus potest de potentia que non potest
de iusticia. Illud enim dicitur non posse de
iusticia quod obviat ordinationi sue
voluntatis vel veritati sue legis . . . sed
illud dicitur posse de potentia absoluta quod
absolute et simpliciter potest quamvis
oppositum ordinaverit vel revelaverit [S I 13
D].

The power to work miracles is part of God's ordained power, provided these are compatible with what He has ordained or revealed. But, according to Peter, God can perform acts incompatible with what He has ordained or revealed; since He is omnipotent, He can do whatever can be done, whatever's being done does not imply a contradiction.

> God is called omnipotent because He can do whatever can be done, that is, everything whose being done does not imply a contradiction.

One can therefore think of God performing actions and consider in these actions solely whether they involve contradictions, that is, solely whether God has the power to perform them, abstracting from all other considerations. For example, for Peter, God can do by this absolute power what is opposed to His justice. His justice is manifested in what He has ordained in the natural order and what He has revealed in the supernatural order. And God's absolute power enables Him to act independently of this, and thus independently of divine justice.

> God can do by His power what He cannot do by His justice. For He is said not to be able to do by His justice what is contrary to what His will has decreed or to the truth of His law, but He is said to be able to do by His absolute power what He can do absolutely and simply, although it is opposed to what He has decreed or revealed.

Et quia potentia intelligitur ut exequens,
voluntas autem ut imperans, et intellectus et
sapientia ut dirigens, quod attribuitur
potentiae secundum se consideratae dicitur
Deus posse secundum potentiam absolutam [St.
Thomas Aquinas, Summa Theologiae, I, 25, 5,
ad 1].

This understanding of divine absolute power seems to be the same as that of St. Thomas Aquinas, for whom God is said to be able to do by His absolute power what He can do absolutely, that is, abstracting from His goodness, His justice, or His wisdom.

And, because power is understood as that which executes, the will however as that which commands, and the intellect and wisdom as that which directs, God is said to be able to do according to His absolute power what is attributed to power considered in itself.

The question is, however, whether God could ever act independently of His goodness, justice, or wisdom. St. Thomas teaches that He could not [ST, I, 25, 5, ad 1-2]. So do St. Bonaventure and William of Ockham [7, pp. 255, 263, 267]. It would seem however that Peter of Ailly thinks that God could do so. For his Commentary on the Sentences can fairly be characterized as a meditation on the absolute power of God; one can hardly believe that Peter would have spent all his time drawing out consequences of the divine absolute power if he thought God could never use it.

Besides, if God never acts by His absolute power, and cannot do so, what does it mean to say God can do something by His absolute power? For Courtenay it means only that it is not a contradiction [7, pp. 267-268]. We are here at a very important point as we prepare to follow Peter of Ailly's unfolding of his

27

philosophy, which consists chiefly of using the notion of God's absolute power to remove necessity from the created universe. For, if God cannot act by His absolute power, what sense does it make to say that what He can do by His absolute power is not a contradiction? How can an impossibility not be a contradiction?

Courtenay says [7, p. 255] that "Ockham used the distinction to point up the contingent, non-necessary character of our world and its relationships." But, if one is talking about God's absolute power, and not simply His unused ordained power, how can what is possible to God's absolute power (and therefore what is really impossible) point up the contingency of our world? For example, if God allowing a human being to deny the first principle is contrary to His wisdom and goodness and therefore impossible, how can saying that it is possible by God's absolute power point up the contingency of the mind's ability to see the truth of the first principle?

Courtenay asserts [7, p. 255] that speculation about God's absolute power was a means of determining the possibility or impossibility of something. But it would be truer to say that it was a means of stating, not determining, this possibility or impossibility. And we shall have to later ask ourselves whether this speculation was a flowering of sound philosophy or merely a weed in the philosophical garden, producing no useful food itself and harming other plants that could have done so.

. . . fides nostra est vera . . . et per
consequens inconveniens esset quod non posset
defendi et probabiliter sustineri. Etiam
frustra laborarent circa studium fidei
fideles catholici et doctores theologi nisi

At this point we should notice that Peter has
contradicted what he said previously. He has just
taught that the human mind, by God's absolute power,
can be mistaken about the first principle. Yet he has
previously claimed that the mind has absolute evidence
concerning the first principle, and that such evidence
cannot be deceived or err. Indeed, it was
distinguished from conditional evidence because the
latter can be deceived or err if God uses His absolute
power. Thus for Peter there really is no distinction
of the sort alleged to differentiate these two kinds of
evidence. But he does not notice that he has
contradicted himself.

The situation would have been even more
serious if Peter had said that the first principle can
be false, but he never says this. He does, however,
consider this possibility. The question arises for
Christians because they believe doctrines which reason
cannot establish. How is it possible for reason to
defend these doctrines if it cannot prove them? Peter
answers that reason can find probable arguments for
them, and that Catholic thinkers have found such
arguments. Christian faith can be defended by reason,
and at least probable arguments can be found for this
faith. Otherwise theology would be a useless study.

Our faith is true and, as a consequence, it
would be unfitting for it not to be able to
be defended and to be sustained with
probabililty. Also, the Catholic faithful
and the theologians who teach would labor in
vain in the study of the faith unless it

31

posset probabiliter ab omni falsitate tueri
[S I 5 A].

Tres opiniones de anima rationali: Una fuit
Alexandri, quod anima intellectiva humana est
forma materialis, generabilis et
corruptibilis . . . . Prima tamen opinio
superius dicta, circumscripta fide et
sequendo apparentiam rationis naturalis,
inter omnes probabilior videretur [47, ch. 6,
pars 1; f. b3rv].

. . . nec oppositum articuli de unitate [the
text has veritate] Dei, nec oppositum
alicuius alterius articuli fidei, potest
probari in lumine naturali [S I 3 EE].

could be protected from all falsity by
probable reasoning.

But Peter is aware that faith seems to
contradict reason on many important points. For
example, for Peter the opinion of Alexander of
Aphrodisias that the intellective soul is not immortal
is more probably true than are other opinions, as far
as natural reason is concerned. Yet it is, according
to faith, false.

There are three opinions concerning the
rational soul. One was Alexander's, that the
human intellectual soul is a material form,
generable and corruptible. . . . The first
opinion however, stated above, would seem to
be the most probable of all, if we leave
faith out of the picture and follow what
appears to natural reason.

However, even though natural reason has many probable
arguments leading to doctrines opposed to faith, it can
never prove any of these doctrines.

Neither can the opposite of the article
concerning the unicity of God, nor the
opposite of any other article of faith, be
proved in the natural light [of our
intellect].

. . . in philosophia seu doctrina
Aristotelis, nulle vel pauce sunt rationes
evidenter demonstrative . . . . Item
sequitur quod philosophia Aristotelis seu
doctrina magis debet dici opinio quam
scientia. Et ideo valde sunt reprehensibiles
qui nimis tenaciter adherent auctoritati
Aristotelis . . . [S I 3 HH].

. . . nullum in fide nostra traditum, imo
nulla, imo hec omnia simul iuncta aut aliqua
de illis, claudunt vel inferunt
contradictionem seu oppositum primi principii,
nec appropinquant sibi, imo infinite distant
ab eo . . . [S I 1 J].

Indeed, nearly everything in philosophy is simply a
matter of opinion. There are very few demonstrative
arguments. Nearly everything in Aristotle's teaching
is opinion, not science.

> There are no, or few, evidently demonstrative
> arguments in philosophy or in the teaching of
> Aristotle. Also, it follows that the
> philosophy or teaching of Aristotle ought
> rather to be called opinion than knowledge.
> And therefore those who cling too tenaciously
> to the authority of Aristotle are very
> reprehensible.

Thus faith does not contradict natural reason. And,
similarly, it does not contradict the first principle.
It does not even come close to doing so.

> No things handed down in our faith (truly
> none, nor all of these put together, nor any
> of them) include or imply a contradiction, or
> the opposite of the first principle. Nor do
> they come close to this; indeed they are
> infinitely removed from it.

Some have said that the first principle holds for all
of creation but not for God. Peter emphatically denies
this. The first principle is universally true.

. . . absurdum esset dicere quod fides catholica concederet aliquam positionem que non posset sine contradictione apparenter sustineri. Hoc enim esset dicere quod fides negat primum principium, sicut blasphemaverunt quidam dicentes primum principium non tenere in divinis. Quicumque autem hoc dixerit, anathema sit [S I 5 P].

. . . licet positio de Trinitate possit sine contradictione apparenter sustineri, tamen quod ipsa . . . non implicet contradictionem, contra protervum non potest evidenter probari . . . [S I 5 P].

. . . numquam debet concedi aliqua contradictoria de eodem verificari ex natura rei nisi ubi cogit auctoritas fidei [S II principium F].

It would be absurd to say that the Catholic
faith would grant any position which did not
appear to be sustained without contradiction.
For this would be to say that faith denies
the first principle, as some have
blasphemously held by saying that the first
principle does not hold in dealing with God.
Let whoever has said this, however, be
anathema.

Though Peter is convinced of this, he admits that it
cannot be proven as concerns the Trinity.

Although the position concerning the Trinity
can apparently be upheld without
contradiction, still it cannot be proved
evidently, against an obstinate objector,
that it does not imply a contradiction.

We can thus see that Peter teaches that faith
does not contradict the first principle. We therefore
should interpret benignly the few texts in which Peter
says that we should not admit that contradictories are
verified of the same thing unless faith forces us to.

It should never be granted that
contradictories are really verified of the
same subject unless where the authority of
faith demands it.

Probatur quia numquam de eadem re . . .
debent concedi contradictoria nisi hoc
habeatur ex scriptura sancta vel ex
determinatione ecclesie vel ex talibus
inferatur [S I 2 Y].

. . . cum difficillimum sit intelligere
contradictoria verificari de eadem re, hoc
non est ponendum nisi solum ubi fides cogit
[S I 2 Y].

This is proved because contradictories should never be granted concerning the same thing unless this is required by Sacred Scripture or by the determination of the Church, or is inferred from these.

Since it is most difficult to comprehend how contradictories can be verified of the same thing, this should not be posited except where faith requires it.

Perhaps Peter here means "seeming contradictories" rather than contradictories. If so, he does not go as far as John of Rodington who, in lecturing on the Sentences at Oxford about 1340, said that, because of the doctrine of the Trinity, we can legitimately doubt the first principle, though we cannot deny it [37, pp. 82-84]. This position was also held by John Buridan (c. 1300 - c. 1360) [16, p. 524].

Nevertheless Peter has taught that God may, by His absolute power, allow us to deny the first principle, even though the principle remains true. And, in doing this, he has destroyed the distinction between absolute and conditional evidence. We can not be sure that God, by his absolute power, is not letting our intellect assent to a first principle that is false. Thus all evidence in the natural order is conditional, which is what John of Rodington said explicitly.

. . . intellectus non potest naturaliter
scire aliquid quin possit dubitare se scire
illud [37, p. 80].

Unde dici potest quod non sum certus
certitudine scientie de hoc vel de illo, sed
communiter sum certus et secundum communem
cursum rerum [37, p. 85].

The intellect cannot naturally know something
in such a way that it cannot doubt that it
knows it.

John says that, even concerning mathematical
conclusions to which we necessarily assent, we can be
mistaken [37, p. 75].

Peter therefore should have concluded with
John that, in the ordinary course of things, we have no
absolute evidence at all.

Whence it can be said that I am not certain
of this or of that with the certitude of
knowledge, but that I have an ordinary
certitude, according to the ordinary course
of things.

. . . Deus dicitur omnipotens quia potest
facere omne factibile, sive omne illud quod
fieri non implicat contradictionem [S I 13
A].

. . . non est evidenter notum Deum esse . . .
quia Deum esse sola fide tenetur (Ad Heb. XI)
[S I 2 S].

THEOLOGICALLY-BASED SCEPTICISM

We have seen that Peter, in reducing man's ability to know natural truths, has based his teaching on a consideration of God's absolute power, God's ability to do whatever is not a contradiction.

God is called omnipotent because He can do whatever can be done, that is, everything whose being done does not imply a contradiction.

We should consider whether this teaching concerning divine omnipotence, which produces for Peter such great effects in philosophy, is itself for Peter a philosophical doctrine, knowable for certain apart from faith, or a theological doctrine, knowable for certain only by faith.

It is clear that the latter is the case. Even the existence of God, for Peter, is not known for sure except by faith.

It is not known evidently that God exists because it is held only by faith that God exists (To the Hebrews, XI).

43

. . . ille processus Philosophi non probat
demonstrative Deus esse. Unde primo dico
quod non [the text omits non] est evidens
evidentia summa aliquid moveri; diceret enim
protervus quia, licet sic appareat, tamen non
sic est. Secundo dico quod, licet esset
evidens aliquid moveri, non tamen illud ab
alio moveri; diceret enim protervus quod
aliqua seipsam movet ad replendum vacuum . .
. . Tertio dico quod . . . non concluditur
movens immobile; diceret enim protervus quod
movetur B et, licet B pro tunc sit movens
immotum, non tamen immobile. Quarto dico
quod non est evidens quod circulatio non sit
possibilis; immo sic est quod est possibilis
diverso genere cause [S I 3 AA; see also S I
3 GG].

44

Aristotle certainly didn't prove it, Peter says; his argument from motion is filled with uncertainties. Peter claims (1) that it is not absolutely certain that motion exists, since a stubborn opponent (the famous medieval protervus) would say that it is only apparent. And Peter agrees with the protervus (2) that the thing moved may not require an efficient cause other than itself, and (3) that, even if the first mover is unmoved in one chain of moving causes, it may still be movable in another respect. Peter also says (4) that the moving causes may be causes to one another mutually, none being first, as can be the case in final causes.

> That argument of the Philosopher does not prove demonstratively that God exists. Thus, first, I say that it is not evident with the highest kind of evidence that something is moved, since an obstinate objector might say that, though it appears to be, it really is not. Secondly, I say that, even if it were evident that something is moved, it is still not evident that it is moved by something else, since the obstinate objector might say that something moves itself in order to fill a vacuum. Thirdly, I say that [the argument] does not conclude with an unmovable mover, since the obstinate objector might say that B is moved and, although B is an unmoved mover at that time, it is not however immovable. Fourthly, I say that it is not evident that mutual causality is not possible; indeed it is the case that it is possible with a different kind of cause.

Diceret enim protervus quod . . . non
evidenter sequitur "A noviter est; igitur ab
aliquo" quia . . . potest incipere esse per
solam absentiam impedientis, nullo ad hoc
positive concurrente [S I 3 GG].

Verbi gratia, tu dicis quod ignis efficit vel
producit calorem . . . . Constat tamen quod
iste calor posset esse, et non esse ab illo
igne sed a solo Deo . . . [S I 3 GG].

Peter also thinks (5) that an effect may be produced not by a cause acting positively but simply by an impediment being removed.

> For the obstinate objector might say "A begins to be; therefore something causes it" does not evidently follow, because it can begin to be simply because of the absence of an impediment, nothing concurring in this in a positive way.

He also, with obvious illogicality, thinks (6) that, since an apparent cause may not be a real cause but may be replaced by God, one may not argue demonstrably from effects to God.

> For example, you say that fire makes or produces heat. It is clear however that this heat could exist but not be from that fire but from God alone.

And Peter continues to pile up objections to an argument seeking to establish the existence of God from the existence of motion. (7) We cannot be sure that efficient causes are essentially ordered (so that the causality of a later cause requires the present causality of an earlier one). (8) We cannot be sure that essentially ordered causes cannot be infinite in number. (9) We cannot be sure that essentially ordered causes are not mutually interdependent, none of them being first [S I 3 GG].

47

. . . "Deus non est" implicat
contradictionem, licet non explicet (id est,
non sit nobis evidens) ipsam inferre
contradictionem [S I 3 Y].

. . . ista consequentia non est evidens,
"Veritas est; ergo Deus est" . . . [S I 3
AA].

. . . licet ista propositio "Deus est" non
sit nobis evidens aut evidenter
demonstrabilis, ipsa tamen est naturaliter
probabilis [S I 3 X].

Nor will Peter accept some type of a priori argument for God's existence. One cannot prove that "God does not exist" implies a contradiction, though several fourteenth-century philosophers [22] said this.

"God does not exist" implies a contradiction, even if it is not explicit (that is, it is not evident to us) that it implies a contradiction.

Nor can one successfully argue that, if there were no truth, it would be true that there was no truth, and thus there would be truth, and thus the First Truth, God, would have to exist.

This argument is not evident: "Truth exists; therefore God exists."

Nevertheless, all in all, despite all these difficulties, Peter thinks that the philosophical argument for God is probable, and that it is even more probable than the argument for the other side.

Although this proposition "God exists" is not evident to us or evidently demonstrable, still it is naturally probable.

. . . licet protervus possit eam [rationem] multipliciter evadere . . . tamen probabilius persuadet quam possit persuaderi oppositum . . . [S I 3 HH].

Et per consequens per istam rationem patet sufficienter, licet non evidenter, quod oportet dare primum conservans et ita primum efficiens [S I 3 HH].

Although the obstinate objector might get around that argument in many ways, still there is greater probability of its persuading than of its opposite being made persuasive.

Peter also thinks that a better argument can be given if one looks for a conserving cause rather than a producing cause. In this, as in many other aspects of his teaching concerning the existence of God, he follows William of Ockham [61, d. 2, q. 10]. Peter uses the premise "Whatever is really produced by another is really conserved by something as long as it remains in real being" [S I 3 HH]. This argument leads to the conclusion that there is a first conserving cause, and hence a first efficient cause, but it still does not, for Peter, prove the conclusion.

And, as a consequence, through this argument it is sufficiently clear, although not evidently, that we should posit a first conserving cause and thus a first efficient cause.

Now, if the existence of God cannot be known with certitude by reason, neither can His attributes. We cannot prove that God is free or that He is active. This is known only by faith.

Sunt enim multe perfectiones simpliciter et
proprietates Dei que pure creduntur ex fide,
vel quas nullo modo est evidens Deo
convenire, sicut esse liberum, activum . . .
[S I 3 CC].

. . . multe rationes naturales possunt fieri
et facte sunt a philosophis concludentes
tantum unum Deum esse, licet non evidenter.
Tamen probabiliter, et probabilius quam
posset concludi oppositum . . . [S I 3 DD].

. . . protervus diceret quod, licet unum
esset tantum primum efficiens, illud tamen
non esset simpliciter primum ens et
perfectissimum quia aliquid esset eo prius
quod non esset efficiens sed eius ultimus
finis propter quod ageret [S I 3 GG].

For there are many qualities simply perfect, and properties of God which are believed purely by faith, or which do not in any evident way belong to God, such as to be free, to be active.

We cannot be sure there is only one God except by faith, though in philosophy it is more probable that there would be one God rather than several.

Many natural arguments can be made, and have been made, by philosophers who conclude, although not with evidence, that there is only one God. Yet this is done with probability, and with greater probability than its opposite can be concluded.

And, even if we knew in philosophy that there was one first efficient cause of all else, we would not know it was the first or most perfect being, because there could be a being above it that would be its final cause and hence prior to it.

The obstinate objector might say that, even though there were only one first efficient cause, it would still not be the first and most perfect being simply speaking, because there would be something prior to it which would not be an efficient cause but the ultimate end on account of which it acted.

53

. . . sicut [the text has sic] probabile est
Deum intelligere, igitur etiam probabile est
ipsum intelligere alia a se [S I 11 K].

. . . omnem entitatem possibilem Deus potest
facere . . . . Probatur . . . auctoritate
scripture sacre quia non potest evidenter
probari ratione [S I 13 E].

. . . non est nobis evidens nec demonstrabile
per rationem aliquam potentiam activam esse
omnipotentem [S I 13 F].

. . . "Deus est omnipotens" . . . est
probabile in naturali lumine. . . [S I 13 F].

Nor can philosophy establish with more than probability that God is intelligent, or that He knows anything other than Himself.

As it is probable that God understands, thus it is also probable that He understands things other than Himself.

Thus we cannot know for sure, except by faith, that God is omnipotent.

God can make every possible being. This is proved by the authority of Sacred Scripture because it cannot be proved by reason with evidence.

It is not evident to us, nor demonstrable by reason, that there is an active power which is omnipotent.

"God is omnipotent" is probable in the natural light [of reason].

From this it becomes clear that Peter's philosophical scepticism is a result not of his philosophy but of his interpretation of Christian faith in the omnipotence of God. It is only because of revelation that Peter will be sure that the created world is constantly trembling

on the verge of being changed drastically or even annihilated.

Having established this point, it is important to comment on Peter's arguments for God's existence. He renders everything problematic. No questions can be answered with anything more than probability. One is astonished to find him saying that the argument for God's existence based on motion is probable. He has raised nine serious and independent objections against it, any of which, if granted, would render it worthless. Yet, without answering any of these objections, he declares the argument for God's existence probable.

It is important also to consider the first and fourth of these objections, which seem to claim that the principle of causality, "Whatever is moved is moved by another", is not universally true. Peter nowhere denies this principle, but here he raises against it two unanswered objections. The weakening of trust in the causal principle redounds not only on the causal argument for God's existence but also on the need for God's universal causality of which Peter makes so much.

Having now considered the lessening of trust in the intellect's power to obtain certainty, and seen that this lessening of trust is due to theological rather than philosophical considerations, we should next see how Peter applies his teaching on certitude in the physical, moral, and supernatural orders.

. . . ex causis naturalibus non potest fieri
quod Sortes sentiat aliquod obiectum quod est
per se obiectum illius sensus quo sentitur,
approximatum in debita distantia, organo bene
disposito et etiam medio, et Sortes iudicet
se non sentire illud obiectum. Patet quia
aliter sensus deciperetur circa proprium
obiectum [S I 1 P].

Verum est tamen quod naturaliter noticia
intuitiva non potest esse sine existentia

THE PHYSICAL ORDER

According to Peter, a sense is a trustworthy means of knowing its proper object. If a sense-object is the right distance from Sortes's sense, and his sense-organ and the medium are properly disposed, he will sense the object there. Otherwise a sense would be deceived concerning its proper object.

It cannot be brought about by natural causes that Socrates sense an object which is the proper object of the sense by which it is being sensed, with the object at the proper distance, and with the sense organ and also the medium properly disposed, and Socrates judge that he does not sense that object. This is evident because otherwise a sense would be deceived about its proper object.

In the order of nature, sensation (a form of intuitive knowledge) can not exist without the existence of its object, which is the direct or indirect efficient cause of sensation.

It is true however that intuitive knowledge cannot exist naturally without the existence

rei, que est vere causa efficiens eius,
mediata vel immediata [S I 3 L].

. . . videtur probabilius quod talis exterior
sensatio non potest naturaliter fieri non
existente sensibili objecto . . . [47, ch.
11, pars 4; f. d2v].

. . . impossibile est viatorem aliquid
extrinsecum ab eo sensibile evidenter
cognoscere esse, evidentia simpliciter
absoluta, sed bene evidentia secundum quid et
condicionata [S I 1 F].

. . . nullum extrinsecum . . . ut puta quod
albedo est, . . . quod homo est alius ab
asino . . . [S I 1 F].

of the thing, which is truly its efficient
cause, mediate or immediate.

It seems more probable that such an external
sensation cannot be produced naturally if the
sensible object does not exist.

But this is true only as concerns conditional evidence,
not absolute evidence, at least as regards an object
outside the person sensing, and in this life.

It is impossible for a wayfarer to know with
evidence that a sensible object outside
himself exists. That is, with evidence
simply absolute. But he can indeed do so
with evidence of a sort, that is,
conditional.

Such a person cannot know for sure, for example, that
whiteness exists or that the man he seems to see is not
really an ass.

Nothing extrinsic as, for example, that
whiteness exists, that a man is different
from an ass.

The reason is that God can do, without secondary
causes, whatever He can do with them. He can preserve
one of two things if the other is destroyed, provided

. . . patet de Dei omnipotentia, quia quicquid Deus potest facere mediante causa secunda . . . potest per seipsum. Et quibuscumque duabus rebus datis, quarum una non est pars alterius, Deus potest unam illarum conservare alia destructa. Et per consequentiam, destructo quolibet sensibili extrinseco, posset conservare in anima sensationem . . . [S I 1 F; see also S I 3 M].

. . . noticia intuitiva rei est talis noticia virtute cuius potest sciri utrum res sit vel non sit . . . et, . . . si esset talis noticia per divinam potentiam conservata, cognosceretur rem non esse . . . [S I 3 K].

one is not part of the other. He can thus preserve a sensation of an object if the object is destroyed, or a sensation of one object if another object is present.

This is evident concerning the omnipotence of God because whatever God can do through the medium of a second cause He can do by Himself. And, if any two things are given of which one is not part of the other, God can conserve one of them when the other is destroyed. And, as a consequence, He can conserve sensation in the soul no matter what extrinsic sensible object is destroyed.

Peter, following William of Ockham verbatim [61, prol., q. 1, Z], calls "intuitive knowledge" the knowledge of a thing which indicates whether a thing exists or does not exist. In the case, then, of sense-knowledge of a non-existing object, the person sensing will know that it does not exist.

Intuitive knowledge of a thing is the knowledge by virtue of which it can be known whether the thing exists or does not exist. And, if such knowledge were to be conserved by divine power, it would be known that the thing does not exist.

Peter does not say, however, how the non-existence of an object sensed intuitively will be communicated to

. . . nulla causa secunda sic est proprie
causa alicuius effectus, nec aliquis effectus
sic ex natura rei sequitur ex aliqua causa
secunda, quod causa necessario inferatur
effectu vel quod effectus necessario
presupponat illam causam. Imo effectus pure
contingenter sequitur ex secunda, et secunda
causa pure contingenter antecedit effectum
suum [S IV 1 E].

the person sensing. And this teaching also contradicts
what he has just said: that in this life we cannot have
absolute evidence of a physical object outside us. If
this sensory knowledge is conditional evidence because
the person sensing cannot be sure whether its object
exists or not, it cannot also be intuitive knowledge,
which gives awareness of whether its object exists or
does not exist.

We must examine later the question to what
extent God might actually interfere with sensation in
this way. But first we should see that Peter's
principle concerning divine power can extend, in the
physical order, beyond the question of whether a
particular sense-object exists. It extends, first, to
the question of efficient causality. For Peter, no
effect is produced by its cause necessarily, if we are
speaking of secondary causes. If A seems to cause B we
cannot infer that A has caused B, or that B has been
caused by A. Because all secondary causes operate by
God's power, and God can produce, without secondary
causes, whatever He produces with them, no effect
follows necessarily from a secondary cause. Every
effect follows purely contingently.

> No secondary cause is properly the cause of
> some effect, and no effect follows naturally
> from a secondary cause, in such a way that
> the cause is necessarily implied by its
> effect or that the effect necessarily
> presupposes that cause. Indeed, an effect
> follows from a secondary cause purely
> contingently, and a secondary cause precedes
> its effect purely contingently.

. . . effectus qui sequitur ad positionem
cause, et hoc ex virtute propria ipsius
cause, non solum sequitur ex voluntate Dei
sed ex natura rei [S IV 1 F].

Tamen quod ad presentiam alicuius cause
secunde sequatur aliquis effectus virtute
ipsius cause seu ex natura rei solum est ex
voluntate Dei [S IV 1 F].

Unde, concurrentibus omnibus causis
requisitis ad hoc quod ignis producat ignem,
potest cum eis agere vel non agere, quia Deus
potest eis coagere vel non coagere [49, col.
632].

This does not imply that secondary causes are not true causes. They are. Their effects are caused by them of their very nature.

> An effect which follows from the positing of a cause, and this from the very power of the cause itself, follows not only from the will of God but from the nature of things.

But that the cause <u>is</u> a cause is due to God's will, not to the nature of the cause. It is God's decision, then, whether a being which of itself is apt to be a cause actually functions as one in a given case.

> However it depends solely on God's will that, at the presence of a secondary cause, an effect follows by virtue of the cause itself or from the nature of things.

> Hence, if all the causes necessary for fire producing fire are present at the same time, it can act with them or not act, because God can be a co-agent or not be a co-agent.

Peter's principle concerning divine power also extends in the physical order to the question of the co-existence of contraries. It is possible by God's absolute power, Peter thinks, for contraries to co-exist in the whole of the same subject at the same

. . . possibile est per divinam potentiam
contraria simul loco et tempore inesse
subiecto secundum se totum, ut quod idem
secundum se totum sit calidissimum et
frigidissimum . . . [S IV 5 BB].

Contraria sunt que non possunt naturaliter
simul inesse eidem . . . .

. . . nulla res est alteri contraria
formaliter et necessario sed solum
naturaliter et de cursu nature a Deo libere
ordinato [S IV 5 BB].

time and in the same place. For example, a body could
be very hot and very cold.

      Through divine power it is possible that
contraries exist in an entire subject in the
same place and at the same time; for example,
that the same thing be completely extremely
hot and extremely cold.

      It belongs to the definition of contraries
that they cannot be <u>naturally</u> in the same subject, that
is, according to the physical order God has freely
established. By God's absolute power however they can
be in the same subject.

      Contraries by definition cannot naturally be
in the same subject at the same time.

      Nothing is formally and necessarily contrary
to another thing, but only naturally and in
the course of nature freely ordained by God.

It is thus possible for a vessel to have two contrary
places, and for it to be full of wine in one place and
empty in the other. And it is possible for a body to
occupy two places and be alive in one and dead in the
other.

Dico tamen ultra quod possibile est idem vas
simul tempore esse in uno loco plenum vino et
in alio vacuum vino . . . .

. . . possibile est etiam idem corpus esse in
uno loco vivum and in alio mortuum . . . [S
IV 5 BB].

. . . Deus sua infinita potentia potest omnem
rem absolutam facere vel conservare sine re
absoluta ab ea secundum se totam realiter
distincta [S IV 5 FF].

Et per consequens potest omnem substantiam
vel qualitatem habentem partem extra partem
facere vel conservare sine omni accidente

70

I say however, further, that it is possible
for the same vase, at the same time, to be
full of wine in one place and to have no wine
in it in another place.

It is also possible for the same body to be
alive in one place and dead in another.

Peter's principle that God can preserve one
of two things if the other is destroyed, provided one
is not part of the other, has a further application in
the question of the relationship between substance and
accident. If two things are really distinct, Peter
says, again following William of Ockham [61, prol., q.
1, HH], God by his absolute power can make or preserve
one without the other.

God by His infinite power can make or
conserve any non-relative thing without
[another] non-relative thing which is really
distinct from it in its totality.

He can make substances without accidents, and accidents
without substances. This does not involve a
contradiction.

And, as a consequence, as regards every
substance or quality having one part outside
another, He can make or conserve [the former]
without any non-relative accident formally

71

absoluto sibi formaliter inherente et sine
omni subiecto cui formaliter inhereat quia
substantiam esse sine accidente, et accidens
sine subiecto, nullam contradictionem
includit [S IV 5 FF].

. . . in creaturis possibilis est
intelligentia quae non sit volitiva, et per
consequens nec libera, sed non econtra . . .
quia Deus potest communicare creaturae
priorem denominationem perfectionis sine
posteriori, et non econtra, quia, cum ita
fit de aliqua, ita posse esse de qualibet non
apparet repugnantia [49, col. 632].

inhering in it, and [the latter] without any subject in which it formally inheres, because a substance existing without an accident, and an accident without a subject, involves no contradiction.

God can make a being without conferring on it further perfection though He cannot make a higher perfection without a lower one which it requires in order to exist. God can not, for example, make an intellect that is not living, or a will without an intellect. But He can make an intellect without a will, since this does not appear to be a contradiction.

In creatures it is possible that there be an intelligence which does not have a will and consequently is not free, but not vice versa, because God can give to a creature a prior class of perfection without a subsequent one, but not vice versa, because, since this is done in regard to some [perfection], it does not seem contradictory for it to be possible of each.

God can also arrange for a body to have some accidents in one place and not to have them in another, at the same time. And for a substance to have a certain whiteness in one place and to have another whiteness in another place. All this is possible, of course, only by God's absolute power.

. . . illud non est necessarium necessitate absoluta quia stat quod de potentia Dei absoluta . . . corpus potest habere aliqua accidentia in uno loco et carere in alio licet in utroque sit circumscriptive . . . .

. . . potest unum subiectum in uno loco esse et ibi habere unam albedinem et esse in alio loco et ibi carere illa et habere aliam. Sed hoc non est possibile naturaliter [S IV 5 ss].

Unde, si illum actum qui est odium Dei in mente dyaboli Deus poneret sine subiecto, tunc non esset odium, sicut nullus eo esset odiens [S I 13 K; see also S I 1 O and S I 3 F].

That is not necessary with absolute necessity because it is possible that, by the absolute power of God, a body can have certain accidents in one place and not have them in another, even though it is in both places circumscriptively.

A subject can be in one place and possess a whiteness there, and be in another place and there lack that whiteness and have another. But this is not naturally possible.

Peter also attributes to God the power to take accidents from an immaterial substance and have them exist outside of a substance. For example, He can make an act of hatred in the Devil's mind have its own existence outside of a subject, though Peter says that it would then cease to be an act of hatred since no one would be hating with it.

Hence if God were to posit, outside of a subject, that act which is [now] an act of hatred of God in the Devil's mind, it would then not be hatred since no one would be hating with it.

Peter seems to want to safeguard the reliability of human knowledge in the case of substance and accident as he does in the case of a sense-object. He says that intuitive knowledge of substances and

Similiter quando alique res intuitive
cognoscuntur, quarum una inheret alteri, vel
una distat loco ab altera, vel alio modo se
habet ad alteram, statim virtute illius
noticie incomplexe scitur si res inheret vel
non, si distat vel non, et sic de aliis
veritatibus contingentibus [S I 13 K].

. . . nulla substantia corporea exterior a
nobis naturaliter est in se cognoscibilis,
quidquid sit de anima intellectiva vel
quacumque alia substantia que est de essentia
cognoscentis. Unde, cum video ignem, eius
substantia non cognoscitur in seipsa quia non
cognoscitur intuitive. Sed de facto non
cognoscitur in se nisi accidens ignis [S I 3
N].

accidents indicates whether accidents inhere in
substances or do not, whether these things are in the
same place or not, and so on, though, again, he does
not indicate how the knower is aware that this is the
case if, for example, an accident exists outside a
substance.

> Similarly, when some things are known
> intuitively, one of which inheres in the
> other, or is spatially apart from the other,
> or is related in some other way to the other,
> it is immediately known, by virtue of that
> incomplex knowledge, whether the thing
> inheres or not, whether it is apart or not,
> and so on concerning other contingent truths.

Yet Peter also says that, with the possible exception
of our own intellective soul, or any substance which is
part of our essence, we cannot naturally know in itself
any physical substance outside ourselves. Only
accidents are known.

> No corporeal substance outside us is
> naturally knowable in itself, whatever might
> be the case with the intellective soul or any
> other substance which is of the essence of
> the knower. Hence, when I see fire, its
> substance is not known in itself because it
> is not known intuitively. But, as a matter
> of fact, only an accident of fire is known in
> itself.

Potest enim facere de creaturis quicquid vult
[S IV 5 FF].

Peter sums up God's absolute power over the physical world, indeed over the whole world of creatures: God can do with them whatever He wants.

Because He can do with creatures whatever He wants.

We thus see that, for Peter, in the physical order, we cannot know in itself any substance except our own. Also, because of God's absolute power, we cannot be sure that the objects of our external senses exist (though, as we have seen, Peter contradicts himself on this) or whether the apparent cause of an effect is its real cause.

These positions were common in the fourteenth century. Many writers held that, because of God's absolute power, we cannot be sure of the existence of any substance except our own soul. For example, Nicholas of Autrecourt (c. 1340) and Richard Fitzralph (1328) held this [19], and in the notebook of Stephen Patrington, O.Carm., a questio says that we cannot know any substances at all (c. 1380) [22]. For the same reason this questio claims that we cannot be sure the objects of our external senses exist. And Nicholas of Autrecourt, Robert Holcot O.P. (1332-33), and John of Rodington (c. 1340) teach that we cannot be sure a secondary cause is producing a particular effect [19; 37, p. 81].

Peter of Ailly also teaches that it is possible by God's power:

1.   That contraries co-exist in the same subject.

2.   That the same body be in two places at once.

3.   That substances exist without accidents, and vice versa.

4.   That an intellective being could exist without a will.

5.   That acts of knowledge and volition exist outside of an intellect or a will.

These or similar teachings were also common in the fourteenth century. For example, John Went O.F.M. (1338-39) and John of Rodington say that contraries can exist in the same subject at the same time [24; 36, p. 82].

We must now see what "God can do with creatures whatever He wants" means for Peter in the moral order.

Nec ideo precipit [Deus] bona quia bona sint,
vel prohibet mala quia mala sint, sed . . .
ideo bona sunt quia precipiuntur, et mala
quia prohibentur [S I 14 B].

. . . nullum est ex se peccatum sed precise
quia lege   prohibitum [S II principium D;
see also S I principium E and S II principium
Q].

. . . nullum est bonum vel malum quod Deus de
necessitate sive ex natura rei diligat vel
odiat . . . .

THE MORAL ORDER

According to Peter, the act of a rational creature is good if commanded by God, evil if forbidden by Him. No act is good or bad of its nature. As a result, the ultimate moral norm is the will of God. This will is ruled by no antecedent moral law. Hence whatever God wills is just.

> God does not command good things because they are good, or forbid evil things because they are evil, but they are good because they are commanded, and evil because they are forbidden.

> Nothing is a sin of itself but precisely because it is prohibited by law.

There is no justice, for example, except what God accepts as justice. God is not just because He loves justice; something is just because God freely so decides.

> There is no good or evil which God loves or hates of necessity or from its very nature.

Nec aliqua qualitas est ex natura rei
iusticia sed ex mera . . . acceptatione
divina. Nec Deus iustus est quia iusticiam
diligit, sed potius econtra aliqua res est
iusticia quia Deus eam diligit, id est,
acceptat [S I 9 R].

. . . nullus actus est meritorius vel
demeritorius essentialiter et intrinsice, sed
solum ex divina acceptatione vel
deacceptatione [S I 9 S].

Unde signum est magne ruditatis et
ineruditionis in scripturis facere magnam
difficultatem in hoc, sicut communiter
faciunt rudes iuriste qui imaginantur Deum
esse oligatu[m] legibus creatis quasi aliquid
per prius sit iustum quam Deus velit illud,
cum tamen omnino sit e converso. Ideo tales
errant [S I 12 J].

Nor is a certain quality, of its nature, justice, but simply from God's accepting it. Nor is God just because He loves justice; on the contrary, rather a thing is just because God loves it, that is, accepts it.

Similarly, no act is essentially and intrinsically meritorious or blameworthy. It depends simply upon whether God accepts it or rejects it.

No act is essentially and intrinsically meritorious or demeritorious, but only from the divine acceptance or rejection.

Peter ridicules those who find it difficult to accept this teaching, and calls them very unlearned in things scriptural.

Hence it is a sign of great ignorance and of a lack of scriptural knowledge to make a big fuss about this, as uncultured jurists always do. They imagine that God is obliged by created laws, as if something were just before God wills it, although the truth of the matter is the exact opposite. Therefore such persons are in error.

Sed teneri est habere a suo superiori prohibitionem vel preceptum de aliquo existente in inferioris libera potestate. Iste autem descriptiones sunt terminorum declarationes. Ideo non possunt probari, sed apparent rationabiles cuilibet recte intuenti [S I principium F].

. . . Deus est pronior ad miserendum quam ad alia opera . . . . Ergo . . . ipsam [creaturam] ratione capacem posset non obligare . . . [S I 14 X].

To be morally bound is to have from one's
superior a precept concerning something within one's
free power. This definition is one that is seen as
correct by anyone who looks at it rightly.

But to be obligated is for a subject,
concerning something in his free power, to
have a prohibition or precept from his
superior. These descriptions however are
definitions of terms; therefore they cannot
be proved, but appear reasonable to anyone
looking at them correctly.

Since right and wrong depend solely on God's
free will, acts of God's will are necessary to create
an obligation. According to Peter, God could perhaps
have left rational creatures without any moral
obligations. This would not have been out of place,
either, since their nature does not of itself require
any special moral order, and one might have thought
that God's goodness would not lay unnecessary burdens
on His rational creatures.

God is more prone to have mercy than to do
anything else. Therefore it would be
possible for Him not to obligate a creature
capable of reason.

Tertio sequitur quod non est evidenter impossibile Deum velle rationalem creaturam esse et ipsam non teneri ad aliquod possibile [S I principiam H].

. . . absolute est possibile rationalem creaturam esse a Deo et ipsam non obligari ab eo . . . .

. . . nulla contradictio apparet quod Deus velit eam esse et non velit eam teneri ad aliquid, sicut de facto est de irrationabili creatura . . . .

Immo, iste due rationes videntur plus concludere: scilicet, attenta misericordia Dei, ipse possit ordinare quod quodlibet factibile a creatura sit consilium ita quod quicquid faciat non solum non sit peccatum, immo meritum. Sed hoc non assero [S I 14 X].

It follows, thirdly, that it is not evidently impossible for God to will that a rational creature exist and yet that it not be bound to something within its power.

Peter is not fully convinced, but suggests that there is no contradiction in God not willing to bind rational creatures with any obligations. Similarly, perhaps God could simply have recommended that rational creatures do certain things and then have rewarded them for doing them. There would then be no moral prohibitions or punishments, only counsels and rewards.

It is absolutely possible for a rational creature to come from God and not be obligated by Him.

There seems to be no contradiction in God willing it to exist and not willing it to be obligated to something, as is actually the case with an irrational creature.

Indeed, these two arguments seem to conclude more: namely, considering the mercy of God, that He can ordain that anything to be done by a creature is a counsel, so that whatever it does is not only not a sin but something meritorious. But I am not asserting this.

. . . ipsa [voluntas divina] de potentia
ordinata non posset rationalem creaturam
obligare nisi mediante aliqua lege creata.
Hoc est per aliqua signa ex quibus sibi
potest innotescere ipsa Dei voluntas
obligatoria [S I principium H].

. . . concedo quod de potentia absoluta stat
creaturam rationalem peccare et committere
vel omittere contra divinum velle et non
contra dictamen alicuius legis create . . .
quia . . . lex creata non potest obligare
sine prima, sed bene prima sine quacumque
alia [S II principium P].

Peter also thinks that, by His ordained power, God cannot oblige rational creatures unless He establishes laws for them, and makes these laws known. His only proof for this need for promulgation, however, is two texts of Scripture.

> The divine will, of its ordained power, could not obligate a rational creature except by means of a created law. That is, through some indications from which God's obligatory will can be made known to it.

By His absolute power, however, God can oblige rational creatures without setting up laws. It is difficult to see what kind of obligation this would be or how rational creatures would know they were obligated, but God could do this because He can do directly whatever He can do indirectly.

> I grant that, as concerns [God's] absolute power, it is possible for a rational creature to sin and to offend against the divine will by commission or omission, without it being against the dictate of a created law, because a created law cannot oblige without the First [Law], but of course the First can without any other.

God has promulgated His laws to human beings in two ways. In the natural order He has given basic

. . . divine voluntatis signa obligatoria
sunt in multiplici differentia. . . . quedam
sunt naturalia seu naturaliter habita; alia
sunt supernaturalia et supernaturaliter data.
Signorum vero naturalium quedam sunt a natura
immediate, sicut prima principia moralia
solum per sinderesim et lumen naturalis
rationis habita. Alia sunt a natura mediate,
sicut conclusiones morales . . . . Sub primo
membro continentur illa principia moralia
quibus unusquisque compos mentis naturaliter
assentit absque eruditione doctorum, ut quod
cuilibet reddendum est quod suum est, quod
nulli iniuriandum est . . . . Signorum autem
supernaturalium quedam sunt a Deo immediate .
. . . Alia sunt a Deo mediate [S I
principium L].

moral principles (called synderesis, or the light of natural reason), such as that a person should be given what belongs to him. From these principles come all the conclusions of natural moral science. In the supernatural order God has spoken to the human race directly.

> There are many kinds of obligatory signs of the divine will. Some are natural, or naturally gained; others are supernatural, and supernaturally given. Now, some of the natural signs are from nature immediately, such as the first moral principles, which are gained by sinderesis and the light of natural reason alone. Others are from nature mediately, such as moral conclusions. In the first group are contained those moral principles to which anyone of sound mind naturally assents without the knowledge of learned men, such as that to each person must be restored what belongs to him, that no one should be wronged. Some of the supernatural signs are from God immediately. Others are from God mediately.

However, God was not bound to choose the laws He chose. By His absolute power He could command us so that we would be bound by another set of laws altogether. This is quite consistent with Peter's teaching that nothing is good or bad in itself except obedience to God. The laws God has put in the deep recesses of our intellect could, by God's absolute power, be set aside. And the

. . . de potentia ordinata non stat creaturam rationalem peccare vel committere aut omittere contra divinum velle et non contra dictamen rationis seu legis nature aut alterius legis create. . . . de potentia absoluta stat creaturam rationalem peccare et committere vel omittere contra divinum velle et non contra dictamen alicuius legis create [S II principium P].

. . . non videtur impossibile nec implicare contradictionem quod Deus posset absolute obligare creaturam ad utendum Deo et fruendum seipsa aut alio obiecto creato [S I 1 N].

same is true of the laws God has revealed to us supernaturally.

> By [God's] ordained power it is not possible for a rational creature to sin, or to offend by commission or omission, against the divine will and not against the dictate of reason or of the law of nature or of some other created law. By [His] absolute power it is possible for a rational creature to sin, and offend by commission or omission, against the divine will and not against the dictate of a created law.

> Since God is quite free, by His absolute power He could command someone to have something other than God as his last end, the person himself or another creature. And God could command that He be an object to be used rather than the purpose of the person's life. At least this doesn't seem to be impossible or to imply a contradiction.

> It does not seem impossible, or imply a contradiction, that God could absolutely oblige a creature to use God and to enjoy itself or some other created object.

> Another important indication of the arbitrariness of the present moral order is that God can command us to hate Him. One might think that, if

. . . non sic est evidenter impossibile Deum
velle ipsam [rationalem creaturam] teneri ad
odium sui . . . [S I principium H].

Patet quia Deus obligat creaturam rationalem
ad obediendum sibi, et tamen Deus non posset
eam obligare ad hoc quod teneatur sibi non
obedire. . . . Et consequentia patet quia
teneri non obedire alicui est teneri ad
aliquid [S I 14 T].

any moral requirement were unchangeable, it would be that we should love God. But Peter says that it is not impossible for God to will to bind rational creatures to hate Him.

> Thus it is not evidently impossible for God to wish a rational creature to be bound to hate Him.

The only divine command which God cannot set aside is the command to obey Him. And the reason Peter gives for this is, not that God is so good that disobedience would be wrong, but that a command not to obey God would involve a contradiction. The one subject to it would obey by disobeying, or disobey by obeying.

> This is clear because God obliges a rational creature to obey Him and yet God could not oblige it to be bound not to obey Him. And the argument is clear because to be bound not to obey someone is to be bound to something.

Apart from this problem of contradiction, God can command anything. No act of a rational creature, even hatred of God, is of itself odious to God. So there is no essential connection between any act and its being rejected by God as not ordained to eternal happiness, or as worthy of eternal punishment.

. . . nec odium Dei nec alius quicumque actus culpabilis est Deo odibilis ex natura rei sive ex sui natura. Patet: nullus talis actus deacceptatur ad vitam eternam vel imputatur ad penam eternam nisi ex mera voluntate divine . . . [S I 9 P].

. . . posset enim una creatura alteri precipere quod odiret Deum. Cum igitur Deus possit per se immediate facere in genere cause efficientis quicquid potest facere mediante causa secunda, et ipse possit mediante creatura tale preceptum facere, sequitur quod per se potest [S I 14 T].

Neither hatred of God nor any other culpable
act is hateful to God from its nature or from
His nature. This is evident because no such
act is rejected for eternal life or ordained
to eternal punishment except from the divine
will alone.

God can give a command that He be hated because He can
do by Himself, as efficient cause, whatever He can do
through the instrumentality of secondary causes. Now,
one rational creature can command another to hate God.
And God would then be the first efficient cause of the
command. So it is not a contradiction for God to give
such a command.

For a creature could command another creature
to hate God. Therefore, since God could in
the order of efficient cause do by Himself
without intermediary whatever He can do with
a secondary cause as intermediary, and He can
make such a command with a creature as an
intermediary, it follows that He can do it by
Himself.

If one were to argue that God, in giving such a
command, would require contrary acts in a person at the
same time, such as love and hate, and that therefore He
can not give such a command, Peter's answer is that
contrary acts are not compossible in the present order
established by God, but are so by God's absolute power.

. . . cum loquamur de potentia absoluta Dei,
non est ad propositum illud quod arguit quod
naturaliter actus contrarii non possunt esse
in eodem [S I 14 U].

. . . non est evidenter impossibile
rationalem creaturam Deum odire et tamen non
[the text omits non; in the Lyons edition
available to me it has been added by hand;
the sense certainly requires it] peccare [S 1
principium H].

. . . quod actus meritorius procedat ex
charitate non est simpliciter necessarium,
sed solum de lege ordinata [S I 14 U].

Tali autem precepto a Deo facto, creatura
obediendo meretur [S I 14 T].

Since we are speaking of God's absolute
power, what [he] argues (that contrary acts
cannot naturally be in the same subject) is
not to the point.

If this is so, however, one wonders why God
could not by His absolute power command rational
creatures even to disobey him. The answer, for Peter,
seems to be that he rules out the possibility of
explicit contradictions (such as obedience and non-
obedience) but not implicit contradictions (such as
love and hate). One could therefore hate God and not
sin.

It is not evidently impossible for a rational
creature to hate God and yet not sin.

Moreover, the act of hatred would be
meritorious. According to the ordained will of God,
merit proceeds from love, but by God's absolute power
it could proceed from hate.

That a meritorious act proceed from charity is
not necessary simply speaking, but only
because of the law that has been established.

When such a command is made by God, however, a
creature merits by obeying.

. . . posset illum articulum restringere ad legem ordinatam, dicendo quod magis factus fuit ille articulus ad reprimendum elatos ne pias aures offenderent quam propter eius falsitatem [S I 14 U; see also S I principium H].

Et probo quod nullam creaturam rationalem potest Deus facere simpliciter impeccabilem . . . . Si quis autem dicat quod Deus posset facere aliquam creaturam rationalem vel liberam [impeccabilem], . . . [respondeo:] tamen dato illi precepto ipsa posset illud non implere quia Deus posset ad impletionem illius sibi non coagere [S I 14 Z].

It is true that in 1347 A.D. the statement "that someone can merit by hating God" was condemned by the theologians of the University of Paris as erroneous, and was listed among the condemned "Parisian articles" [2, p. 611]. But one could simply say that the statement is valid, but only as concerns the ordained will of God, not as concerns His absolute power.

> He could restrict that article to the law laid down, saying that it was made an article in order to restrain the headstrong from offending pious ears rather than because of its falsity.

A person can also be bound to an action from which God could withhold His co-causality, and the person could thus sin without it being his fault.

> And I prove that God cannot make any rational creature, simply speaking, impeccable. . . . If however someone were to say that God could make a rational or free creature impeccable, I answer that, after a precept is given to it, it could still fail to carry it out because God could withhold from it His co-action in its being carrying out.

Moreover, God can by Himself take away from a created will its conformity with God's will.

. . . conformitatem sive rectitudinem voluntatis create Deus potest ab ea auferre quia Deus ab alia auferre potest quamlibet rem que non est eius pars nec e contra [S I 13 J].

. . . Deus non potest auferre rectitudinem voluntatis, ipsa invita. Non quod hoc sit simpliciter impossibile . . . sed quod hoc est impossibile secundum legem statutam [S I 13 J].

> God can take away from a created will its
> conformity or rectitude because God can take
> away from any thing another thing which is
> not part of it or of which it is not a part.

> This is not possible in the present dispensation, but
> it is possible by God's absolute power.

> God cannot take away a will's rectitude if it
> is unwilling. Not that this is impossible
> simply speaking, but that it is impossible
> according to the law that has been laid down.

It is clear that Peter does not have a doctrine of natural law as ordinarily understood, a doctrine that there is an unchanging body of moral principles flowing from human nature. One might argue, as McDonnell has done, that for Peter moral law is unchanging because rational creatures must always obey God [34, p. 392], even though the content of this obligation may change. But this is to have such a minimalistic notion of natural law that the term ceases to be useful. It also fails to recognize that, according to Peter, God could create rational beings who have no moral obligations. These points are well brought out by Oakley, who has also shown that Peter's moral theory comes from William of Ockham [39].

We thus conclude that Peter does not have a natural law theory of morality but rather teaches:

1. That no human act is good or evil in itself.

2. That "good" means "commanded by God," and "evil" means "forbidden by God."

3. That no act is intrinsically meritorious or blameworthy.

Also, by his absolute power, God can bring it about:

4. That human beings not be bound by moral laws.

5. That they be bound without God making this obligation known.

6. That the moral law be changed, even completely, except that human beings must obey God if they are commanded to do so.

7. That God not be man's last end.

8. That human beings sin, or that human wills lose their conformity to God's will, without their fault.

These or similar teachings were common in the fourteenth century. One finds most of them, for example, in the Sentences of John Went, O.F.M., composed at Oxford, 1338-39 [24].

THE SUPERNATURAL ORDER

Having seen the contingency of the physical and moral orders, it is time to see that for Peter there is extensive contingency in the supernatural order also. He thinks that God has established such an order, over and above the natural one. But he also thinks that it could have been very different from what it is, and that by God's absolute power almost any kind of supernatural order was possible.

The importance of seeing the effects of Peter's teaching in the supernatural order is twofold. First, it is important for the history of theology. It can give an indication of the state of theology in the pre-Reformation period, helping to explain not only why there was a Reformation but why it had some of the features it had. But we are not concerned here with this aspect of Peter's teaching.

Second, it is important in showing how a theory of natural knowledge is bound to have consequences concerning the possibility and nature of supernatural knowledge. And this is the aspect of Peter's teaching which is important here. Philosophical scepticism leads to theological scepticism.

Sicut sola divina voluntas respectu
contingentis futuri potest esse causa
inimpedibilis, sic solus divinus intellectus
respectu veri de futuro contingenti potest
esse noticia infallibilis [S I principum Q].

. . . solus divinus intellectus respectu veri
de futuro contingenti potest esse noticia
infallibilis iudicii [S IV principium H; see
also S III principium H; S I 1 P; S I 11 M;
and S I 11 R].

Let us begin with God's knowledge of future contingent events. Peter thinks that many future events are not necessary but are truly contingent. Moreover God, from all eternity, has an infallible knowledge of all such events. Peter does not explain why this is so, but accepts it, along with divine omnipotence, as a doctrine of his Catholic faith. This teaching, then, belongs to the order of revelation, the supernatural order.

As only the divine will, in respect to a contingent future event, can be an unimpedible cause, so only the divine intellect, in respect to the truth about a future contingent event, can be infallible knowledge.

Concerning the truth about a future contingent event, only the divine intellect can be knowledge of an infallible judgment.

As far as God's ordinary power is concerned, then, these events will take place as God forsees them. And, if God has revealed them, as He has revealed that Antichrist will come, and that there will be a final judgment, Christians may be certain that these events will take place.

Prima ergo conclusio erit quod verorum contingentium de futuro est possibilis intellectui creato vera revelatio. Secunda conclusio erit quod . . . est possibilis . . . certa [the text adds <u>vel infallibilis</u>, but this is an obvious mistake] revelatio [S I 12 P; see also S IV principium J].

. . . dicitur quod impossibile est de potentia ordinata ultimum iudicium non fore quia . . . non stat cum eterna Dei ordinatione et obviat sacre scripture [S I 13 D].

. . . ex eo sequitur quod de necessitate Deus aliquid ageret ad extra, imo quod omnia de necessitate evenirent, quod est contra fidem [S I 12 R].

Therefore the first conclusion will be that it is possible for there to be true revelation to a created intellect concerning contingent truths about the future. The second conclusion will be that certain revelation is possible.

As concerns [God's] ordained power, it is said that it is impossible that there be no Last Judgment, since this would be inconsistent with God's eternal decree and contradicts Sacred Scripture.

However, the situation is different as regards God's absolute power. Here the radical contingency of future contingents is retained. This seems quite incompatible with the divine infallible foreknowledge of all future contingents, though Peter does not explicitly point this out. No doubt he didn't want to say openly that he was denying a doctrine of his faith, or even that the doctrine was to be asserted only of what God has actually ordained. But he felt constrained to hold this new position because he was concerned that, if God knew what was going to happen, His knowledge would be necessitated. That is, God would then not be free to have things happen otherwise. All would be necessitated; and this is against faith.

It follows from that that God would perform an action outside Himself of necessity, indeed that all things would happen of necessity, which is against Faith.

. . . sequitur diminutio potentie divine [S I
12 R].

. . . quelibet propositio singularis de
futuro est determinate vera vel falsa . . .
[S I 11 B].

. . . non facilius potest salvari futurorum
contingentia, sive quod futura contingenter
sint futura, non ponendo Dei prescientiam
quam ipsa posita. Nec ipsa prescientia
aliquo modo infert necessitatem in futuris
plus quam possit inferri ipsa non posita . .
. quia, cum quelibet propositio sit
determinate vera, ex hoc ita difficulter
potest argui contra contingentiam futurorum
sicut posita Dei prescientia . . . [S I 11
R].

114

And thus God's power would also be reduced.

A lessening of divine power is a result.

Peter points out, however, that it is not just God's foreknowledge that would remove the contingency of the future. This contingency is also threatened by the fact that present statements about the future are now either true or false. That is, though we do not know how the future will be, it is going to be however it is going to be. Any statement about how it will be is, right now, either true or false. So, for Peter, the doctrine of divine foreknowledge is not the real problem.

Any singular proposition about the future is determinately true or false.

The contingency of future events, or that future events are contingently future, can not be more easily saved by not positing God's foreknowledge than by positing it. Nor does foreknowledge itself in some way imply necessity in future events, any more than necessity can be inferred with foreknowlege not posited, because, since every proposition [every true proposition about a future contingent] is determinately true, it is as difficult to argue from this against the contingency of future events as it is by positing God's foreknowledge.

Ideo fatuum est et signum ignorantie magne in
ista materia negare Dei prescientiam propter
futurorum contingentiam [S I 11 R].

Sicut negatio et privatio, sic nec preteritio
nec futuritio potest effici a Deo . . . quia
nullum tale est entitas sive effectus
causalitatis [S I principium T].

. . . ista oratio "esse futuri" pro nullo
supponit plus quam ista, "esse nihili vel
chymere." Ideo per nullam causam ponitur
aliquid in esse futuri [S I principium S].

He even ridicules those who see it as a problem.

> Therefore to deny God's foreknowledge to
> safeguard the contingency of future events is
> foolish, and a sign of great ignorance in
> this matter.

But had Peter said that present statements about future
contingents are now neither true nor false, as Boethius
said [In . . .Peri Hermeneias, III, 9 (Leipzig, 1880)
p. 215, 11. 21-26], he would have had to admit that how
God knows their truth status now is one of the most
impenetrable of all mysteries.

For Peter, God does not foresee the future as
a result of Him having willed that such and such will
happen, and this for two reasons. First, future
contingents are nothing, and so are not entities on
which God could work. They are like privations, or
nothings, or chimeras.

> Like negation and privation, neither pastness
> nor futurity can be brought about by God
> because no such thing is a being, or an
> effect of causality.

> This expression "the being of a future thing"
> stands for nothing, any more than does this,
> "the being of nothingness or of a chymera."
> Therefore something is not given "the being
> of a future thing" by any cause.

. . . hec opinio deficit . . . specialiter in
hoc quod dicit voluntatem . . . esse rationem
cognoscendi quia, si per impossibile Deus non
esset volens, tamen esset intelligens [S I 11
N].

. . . cum inter intellectum et voluntatem Dei
nulla possit prioritas seu quamvis distinctio
ex parte rei assignari, igitur non est verum
quod sua volitio sit [the text has sicut]
ratio assentiendi intellectui divino . . . [S
III principium F; see also S IV principium
E].

Second, they are not known as a result of God deciding how He will will them to be. Though everything that happens requires an act of God's will, He never decides a future contingent in advance but only in the instant in which it comes to be. God would know future contingents even if (speaking per impossibile) He had no will.

This opinion is deficient especially in saying that the will is that by which knowledge takes place because, if (assuming what is impossible) God did not have a will, He would still be intelligent.

Also, there is no priority or distinction between the divine intellect and the divine will. So the will does not account in any way for the intellect's knowledge.

Since no priority or any distinction can be assigned between God's intellect and will insofar as these things themselves are concerned, therefore it is not true that His will is that by which the divine intellect assents.

God knows future contingents simply because, without any reference to decisions of His will, He knows everything most certainly all at once.

. . . intellectualis et eternus oculus Dei
est quedam intuitio que immediate super
quamlibet rem actualiter vel potentialiter
existentem simul fertur [S I 11 N].

. . . hec est contingens, "Deus revelavit
Sorti quod dies iudicii erit," etiam postquam
revelavit . . . [S I 12 P].

. . . Deus voluit et iudicavit ab eterno
Antichristum fore, et tamen potest numquam
hoc voluisse aut iudicasse, sicut possibile
est Antichristum non fore [S I principium Q;
see also S I 11 R].

The eternal eye of God's intellect is an intuition which is carried at the same time, without intermediary, over everything that exists actually or potentially.

Now, if future contingents are fully contingent until they happen, they remain so even if God reveals them. For example, absolutely speaking, there may not be a Day of Judgment even though God has revealed that there will be.

Even after He has revealed it, this proposition is contingent: "God has revealed to Sortes that there will be a Day of Judgment."

It is possible that Antichrist will not come, even though God has willed and judged from eternity that Antichrist will come.

God willed and judged from eternity that Antichrist will exist, and yet it is possible that He never willed or judged this, since it is possible that Antichrist will not exist.

Accordingly, it follows that, since revelation cannot be infallible, it can be false.

Bene tamen concedendum est quod Sortes qui
vere iudicavit ultimum iudicium fore potest
non iudicasse verum [S I principium Q].

. . . quelibet noticia creata que fuit
revelatio alicuius veri de contingenti adhuc
futuro potest non esse, et numquam fuisse,
revelatio. Patet, supposito quod iste
terminus revelatio importet quod sit assensus
verus et de vero [S I 12 R].

It would have to be granted however that Sortes, who truly judged that there will be a Last Judgment, can not have judged what is true.

In such a case it should not really be called revelation because revelation implies truth.

It is possible that some created knowledge, which was revelation of a truth concerning a still future contingent event, not be, or never have been, revelation. This is evident if we suppose that this term "revelation" implies that it is true assent to what is true.

We can still say nevertheless that the certitude of the revelation was indeed certitude. The word "certitude" can have two meanings. The first involves assent to what cannot be otherwise (and revelation about a future contingent cannot give certitude in this sense). But the second meaning involves a firm assent for a good reason, though one could be wrong. One is right in being certain, since confidence in God's word is justifiable. But the certitude can be deception. And it can never be infallible.

. . . certitudo potest capi dupliciter. Uno modo improprie, ut certificare importat firmiter idem quod assentire alicui complexo et quod non potest aliter esse. Et isto modo satis constat quod Deus non potest certificare aliquem de aliquo vero de contingenti futuro. Alio modo potest certitudo capi proprie ut certificare importat idem quod firmiter assentire alicui complexo vero. Et isto modo satis patet quod, licet non sit possibile quod certitudo sit falsa, tamen certitudo potest esse deceptio . . . . Et ideo ille qui fuit certus post non fuisse certus, et illa noticia que fuit certitudo potest fuisse deceptio et non certitudo [S I 12 P].

. . . non est possibilis . . . infallibilis revelatio [S I 12 P; see also S III principium H].

. . . fidei possibile est subesse falsum. Patet quia istud quod de facto subest fidei potest esse falsum [S I 12 Q; see also S IV principium K].

Sed non sufficeret ad salvandum illam fidem esse noticiam infallibilem . . . [S IV principium J].

Certitude can be taken in two ways. In one way, improperly, as "to be certain" implies exactly the same as "to assent to a judgment which cannot be otherwise". And in this way it is sufficiently evident that God cannot make anyone certain about a truth dealing with a contingent future event. In another way certitude can be taken properly so that "to be certain" implies exactly the same as "to assent to a true judgment". And in this way it is sufficiently clear that, although it is not possible that the certitude be false, still the certitude can be deception. And therefore he who was certain can later not have been certain, and that knowledge which was certitude can have been deception and not certitude.

Infallible revelation is not possible.

        This means that the Christian faith can contain errors.

It is possible for something false to be part of Faith. This is evident because what as a matter of fact is part of Faith can be false.

But it would not be able to make that faith be infallible knowledge.

. . . nego ultra illam consequentiam
"Iudicium non erit; ergo talis ex fide false
iudicavit." Sed bene concedo "Ergo false
iudicavit" [S I principium Q].

Aliqui tamen concedunt quod Christus non
solum potest asserere falsum sed et hoc potest
facere cum intentione fallendi, id est
asserere falsum scitum esse falsum, imo
dicere falsum mendacium, et peccare, odire
Deum . . . . Nec video quin istud possit

Peter prefers however to say that false judgments can
be made in matters of faith but that they do not come
through faith. But this is a purely verbal point.

> Furthermore, I deny that argument "There will
> be no Judgment; therefore such a person
> through faith judged falsely." But I
> certainly grant "Therefore he judged
> falsely."

Peter claims that God cannot reveal future
contingents infallibly, even to Christ in His human
nature. And thus Christ can make false statements. He
can do this even with the intention of deceiving, just
as He can sin, and hate God. These are possible
because the actions of Christ's human nature are
attributed to the divine Person performing them, and
His human nature can do, united to the divine Person,
what it could do if it were not united. At least this
is more probable than its opposite, though Peter fears
it will not sound quite right to most Catholics. They
simply do not understand that one can abstract from
what God has done, and can consider what is possible by
God's absolute power.

> Some however grant that Christ not only can
> assert what is false but also can do this
> with the intention of deceiving; that is,
> assert a falsehood known to be a falsehood,
> indeed utter a lying falsehood, and sin, and
> hate God. Nor do I see, if it does not

probabilius dici quam oppositum si non
offendat aures fidelium. Nulla enim
contradictio vel repugnantia videtur quod
anima Christi absolute omnia possit Verbo
unita que ipsa posset si esset a Verbo
derelicta [S 1 12 Y].

. . . debet intelligi et exponi de
impossibilitate et necessitate secundum legem
ordinatam et non de absoluta impossibilitate
. . . [S I 12 Y; see also S IV principium J].

Et hec via inter alias mihi videtur magis
probabilis quam illa que poneret quod
quelibet noticia creata anime Christi vel
alterius in Verbo sit noticia infallibilis [S
I 12 Y].

offend the ears of the faithful, but that
this can be said with greater probability
than its opposite. For Christ's soul being
absolutely capable, united to the Word, of
all the things it could do if it were
deserted by the Word, does not seem to be a
contradiction or an impossibility.

It ought to be understood and explained as
concerning impossibility and necessity
according to the ordained law, and not
concerning absolute impossibility.

Peter thinks that this position is more probable than
the one claiming that Christ's human knowledge of
contingent futures is infallible.

And, among other positions, this one seems to
me more probable than the one which holds
that some of the created knowledge of the
soul of Christ or of someone else in the Word
is infallible knowledge.

The same is the case with revelation made to
angels. While the Angel Gabriel was on his way to Mary
to announce that God wanted her to be the mother of His
Son, it was possible that Gabriel was mistaken, that he
made a false announcement. Of course he would not have
been a liar, because he would have announced what he
thought was the truth. And all this was possible, of
course, only by God's absolute power.

Unde patet quod pro illo tempore medio, licet
non de potentia ordinata tamen de potentia
absoluta, hoc erat possibilis: Gabriel in
Verbo false iudicavit; Gabriel false
annuntiavit. Nec tamen propter hoc sequitur
quod hec esset possibilis, "Gabriel mentitus
fuit, vel mendax nuncius extitit". . . .
Ratio est quia non dixisset aliquid contra
suam conscientiam, quod requiritur ad
mendacium [S I 12 V].

. . . securitas de eternitate beatitudinis
est pars beatitudinis [S I 12 AA; see also S
I 1 P].

. . . Deus potest rationali creature
securitatem sue eterne beatitudinis revelare
. . . . Et istud est fide tenendum . . . [S
I 12 BB].

Hence it is clear that, for the time in-
between, although not by [God's] ordained
power but by [His] absolute power, this was
possible: Gabriel was mistaken; Gabriel
judged falsely in the Word; Gabriel announced
falsely. And yet it does not follow for this
reason that this was possible: Gabriel lied,
or was a lying messenger. The reason is that
he would not have said something against his
conscience, which is required for a lie.

Since no revelation is infallible, the
Blessed in heaven do not know for sure that they will
remain there. Nevertheless, they must think so, or
their happiness, being insecure, would not be perfect.

Security about eternal beatitude is a part of
beatitude.

So God reveals to each of the Blessed that their
beatitude is secure, as Catholic faith teaches.

God can reveal to a rational creature the
security of its eternal beatitude. And this
must be held by faith.

Yet, since no revelation is infallible, no revelation
being evident knowledge, God can annihilate any of the
Blessed and take away their beatitude.

. . . Deus quemlibet beatum, et de sua beatitudine eterna assecuratum, potest annihilare et ei suam beatitudinem potest auferre . . . .

. . . . concedo quod nulla revelatio de futuro est de illo evidens scientia . . . [S I 12 BB; see also S I 1 P].

. . . ponam probabiliter aliquas propositiones . . . .

. . . isti termini "decipere, fallere, et huiusmodi" dupliciter possunt accipi. Uno modo ut includunt . . . "iniuste, inordinate, indebite." Alio modo ut non includunt ea . . . . Accipiendo tamen primo modo istos terminos, clarum est quod Deus non potest decipere vel fallere . . . . Sed secundo modo illud est dubium, nec est clare sacre scripture contrarium [S I 12 GG; see also S IV principium K].

God can annihilate any one of the Blessed even if he has been assured of His eternal beatitude, and can take away his beatitude from him.

I grant that no revelation about the future is evident knowledge about it.

We must therefore conclude that probably God can deceive. We must here remove from the word "deceive" the suggestion that the deceit is unjust or inordinate. But, having done that, we must say that it is possible that God can deceive.

I will posit, with probability, some propositions.

These terms "deceive, mislead, etc." can be taken in two ways. In one way, as they include "unjustly, inordinately, improperly." In another way, as they do not include them. Taking these terms now in the first way, it is clear that God cannot deceive or mislead. But, in the second way, that is doubtful, nor is it clearly contrary to Sacred Scripture.

God cannot deceive by His ordinary power, but He can do so by His absolute power. For this does not involve a contradiction, as saying "God is not God" does.

. . . Deus non potest de potentia ordinata rationali creature falsum dicere vel eam decipere, et hoc per seipsum immediate et directe [S I 12 HH].

. . . Deus potest de potentia absoluta rationali creature falsum dicere, et eam decipere, etiam per seipsum immediate et directe [S I 12 HH].

Nec ad hoc apparet mihi contradictio, sicut quod Deus non sit Deus . . . [S I 12 HH].

. . . non sequitur Deum esse causam peccati, licet errorem immediate causaret et aliquem deciperet [S I 12 HH].

. . . potest dici quod, si alicui concederetur auctoritate divina, posset mentiri . . . . Et per consequens, si Deus per seipsum immediate alicui falsum diceret cum intentione fallendi, et illo modo mentiretur, non peccaret. Hoc autem est possibile de potentia absoluta . . . [S I 12 JJ].

God cannot, by [His] ordained power, and by Himself immediately and directly, tell a falsehood to a rational creature, or deceive it.

By [His] absolute power, God can tell a falsehood to a rational creature, and deceive it, even by Himself immediately and directly.

Nor does there seem to me to be a contradiction in this, as that God is not God.

This would not imply that God is the cause of sin in His creatures. Error is not sin. God can deceive without causing sin.

It does not follow that God is the cause of sin, even though He were to cause error without an intermediary, and deceive someone.

It can be said that a person could lie if it were permitted him by divine authority. And, as a consequence, if God were to speak a falsehood by Himself immediately with the intention of deceiving, and were to lie in that way, He would not sin. This however is possible by [God's] absolute power.

Sed teneri est habere a suo superiori
prohibitionem vel preceptum de aliquo
existente in inferioris libera potestate [S I
principium F].

. . . restringo omnia inferius dicenda ad
libertatem contingentiae. Et, licet non sit
evidens in naturali lumine talem libertatem
esse, tamen eam esse ponendam suppono ex fide
[49, col. 630].

Peter concludes his treatment of God's power to deceive all his rational creatures by a peroration [S I 12 LL] showing that Christian faith can be false (Antichrist may not come, there may be no Last Judgment), that people may be saved by believing what is false or damned by believing what is true, and that the prophets and Christ may have been mistaken when they told of the future.

Having considered God's knowledge of future contingents in general, let us now see how it affects a particularly important question: the freedom of human beings, and their eternal destiny. We have seen that, for Peter, God is free. But human freedom seems to be eliminated. It is true that Peter sometimes speaks of human freedom, which for him is implied in the very notion of moral obligation. He does not think that freedom can be proven philosophically, but that it is a doctrine of Christian faith that human beings are free.

But to be bound is for a subject to have, concerning something existing in his free power, a prohibition or precept from his superior.

I restrict everything to be said below to the freedom of contingency. And, although it is not evident in the natural light that there is such freedom, nevertheless I suppose from faith that it is to be posited.

. . . Deus nullum . . . predestinat . . .
propter aliquod bonum aut aliquam causam
previsam in predestinato [S I 12 C].

Tunc arguo sic: tale bonum quod tu assignas
est partialis effectus predestinationis; ergo
Deus non propter illud predestinat [S I 12 C;
see also S I 12 L].

. . . iustificatio non est predestinatio sed
predestinationis effectus [S I 12 J].

. . . non habere finalem perseverantiam . . .
est effectus reprobationis . . . [S I 12 B].

Quemcumque Deus reprobavit, sine quacumque
causa in ipso reprobato eum reprobavit [S I
12 G].

Yet he also teaches that human beings are predestined to heaven or reprobated to hell, even in the present dispensation, by God's eternal decree, irrespective of their merits.   It is true that those who are predestined gain merit, and that those who are reprobated have demerits, at least according to the present dispensation, but these merits or demerits are the result, not the cause, of predestination or reprobation.

God predestines no one because of some good or some other cause foreseen in the person predestined.

Then I argue thus: such a good as you assign is a partial effect of predestination; therefore God does not predestine because of it.

Justification is not predestination, but an effect of predestination.

Not to have final perseverance is an effect of reprobation.

Whomever God had reprobated, He has reprobated him without any cause in the person reprobated.

. . . licet predestinatio Dei sit necessaria,
tamen Deus non necessario vel inevitabiliter
sed contingenter est predestinatio. Et ita
dici potest de reprobatione [S I 12 D].

. . . quelibet rationalis creatura a Deo
predestinata potest non esse et numquam
fuisse predestinata [S I 12 C].

Peter therefore seems to want to have radical contingency and no human freedom. Both of these are involved in his exaggerated notion of divine freedom. Peter does not want to have the future decided until it becomes present, so that God may be always free in regard to it. And he wants to remove human freedom so that there may be no obstacle to the divine will. He does not make this latter point explicitly, however. An earlier study has shown how two English philosophers, a few decades before Peter, taught these doctrines so as to safeguard divine omnipotence. Nicholas Aston held that human beings are awarded eternal happiness or misery independent of their merits or demerits. Thomas Buckingham held that God's knowledge of future contingents is uncertain [21]. Now, Peter teaches both of these doctrines. They are incompatible with each other, however, because, if God determines human behavior, a great deal of the future ceases to be contingent. However, Peter wants to have things both ways. Though human beings are predestined or reprobated, the predestination and reprobation somehow remain contingent.

> Though God's predestination is necessary, still God is predestination not necessarily or inevitably, but contingently. And the same can be said of reprobation.

> It is possible for any rational creature predestined by God not to be, and never to have been, predestined.

141

. . . amicis Dei numquam datur Spiritus
Sancti persona quin detur aliquid eius donum
creatum, scilicet caritas vel gratia, nec
similiter econtra [S I 9 D].

. . . amicis Dei absolute potest dari
Spiritus Sancti persona absque hoc quod
dentur eius dona, et similiter econtra [S I 9
D].

He does not explain whether God's absolute power is involved in one of the predestined never having been predestined, but presumably he is claiming that, if He wishes, God could undo an eternal decree of predestination.

In addition to this teaching concerning divine foreknowledge, Peter holds that grace, an infused gift which makes a person pleasing to God, could, by God's absolute power, have very different relationships to the Holy Spirit, faith, hope, friendship with God, guilt, mortal sin, merit, and eternal life, than it has now.

1. By God's ordinary power the friends of God receive the Holy Spirit, Who is always accompanied by grace and charity.

    The person of the Holy Spirit is never given to the friends of God without one of His created gifts being given, namely charity or grace; nor, likewise, vice versa.

    By God's absolute power the Spirit can be given without grace and charity, and vice versa.

    Absolutely speaking, the person of the Holy Spirit can be given to the friends of God without His gifts being given, and also vice versa.

. . . gratia de potentia Dei absoluta potest
infundi sine aliis virtutibus theologicis,
scilicet fide et spe. Patet quia caritas est
quid absolutum quod non dependet a fide et
spe [S IV 3 D].

. . . probabilius est quam oppositum quod
gratia de lege ordinata non potest infundi,
seu non infunditur, in baptismo sine fide et
spe. Patet quia non videtur rationabile quod
Deus unam infunderet sine aliis [S IV 3 D].

Nullus potest esse amicus Dei de lege
ordinata non habendo in se aliquam
qualitatem infusam que sit caritas vel gratia
[S I 9 H].

2. By God's absolute power, grace and charity can be infused without faith and hope being infused, since they are, absolutely speaking, not faith or hope.

    By God's absolute power, grace can be infused without the other theological virtues, namely faith and hope. This is evident because charity is something absolute, which does not depend on faith and hope.

    Admittedly, it would be unreasonable of God to allow this, but it is still possible.

    As concerns the law that has been established, it is more probable than the opposite that in baptism faith cannot be infused, or is not infused, without faith and hope. This is evident because it does not seem rational that God would infuse one without the others.

3. By God's ordinary power, no one can be a friend of God unless he possesses grace and charity.

    By the law that has been established, no one can be a friend of God without having in himself some infused quality, that is, charity or grace.

145

. . . aliquis potest esse amicus Dei de potentia absoluta non habendo aliquam qualitatem infusam que sit caritas vel gratia.

. . . aliquis potest esse non-amicus Dei de potentia absoluta habendo aliquam qualitatem infusam que sit caritas vel gratia [S I 9 H].

. . . gratia et peccatum sive culpa non sunt proprie contraria quia gratia, quo ad omne illud quod est in ea positivum et absolutum, potest stare cum qualibet culpa, et hoc de potentia Dei absoluta. Sed tunc non esset gratia, id est non faceret tunc aliquem esse gratum Deo. Quod igitur gratia repugnet culpe non est naturaliter sed libere, scilicet ex voluntate Dei libere acceptantis talem qualitatem ut faciat aliquem gratum,

146

But, by God's absolute power, one can be a friend of God without them. And, indeed, a non-friend of God with them.

By [God's] absolute power, someone can be a friend of God without having an infused quality, that is, charity or grace.

By [God's] absolute power, someone possessing an infused quality, that is, charity or grace, can be not a friend of God.

4. Similarly, in the order God has established, grace and guilt are contraries. But, by God's absolute power, they can co-exist (of course, grace would not then make its possessor pleasing to God). The reason is that grace is not of its nature opposed to guilt. God has freely chosen to make it so.

Grace, and sin or guilt, are not contraries properly speaking because grace, as regards everything positive and absolute in it, can exist with some guilt; this is by God's absolute power. But then it would not be grace, that is, it would then not make someone pleasing to God. Therefore, that grace is opposed to guilt is not a matter of nature but of choice, that is, from the will of God freely accepting such a quality as making someone pleasing [to Him]. This is

cum quo non stat ipum esse in peccato, sicut
non stat quod sit amicus et inimicus Dei [S
IV 3 G].

. . . caritati infuse et eius actui cupiditas
actualis mortalis est contraria et
incompossibilis. Et capio contrarietatem
large prout illa dicuntur contraria que de
lege ordinata non possunt eidem simul inesse,
sed bene successive, quamvis hoc non sit de
ipsorum intrinseca ratione [S I 9 HH].

. . . dico quod actus peccati mortalis,
scilicet actus adulterii, et actus meriti
vite eterne, scilicet actus confessionis vel
dilectionis Dei super omnia, possunt esse
simul tempore in eodem . . . [S IV 5 CC].

then not compatible with him being in sin, as it is not compatible for him to be the friend and the enemy of God.

Also, mortal sin and infused charity, though in the present dispensation they are contraries, are not so of their very nature.

A mortal sin of cupidity is contrary to infused charity and its act, and not co-possible with it. And I take contrariety in the large sense, in which those things are said to be contrary which, by the law which has been ordained, cannot be in the same subject at the same time, though they can be successively. This however is not of the intrinsic nature of contraries.

Thus an act mortally sinful, and an act meriting eternal life, can be in the same person at the same time.

I say that an act of mortal sin, for example an act of adultery, and an act meritorious of eternal life, for example an act of the praise or the love of God above all things, can be in the same person at the same time.

Nam Deus absolute posset, manente obligatione
ad penam eternam, infundere gratiam et
dimittere culpam, sine iniusticia, sicut
posset aliquem eternaliter punire sine
demerito . . . [S IV 3 G].

. . . etiam si Deus aliquam creaturam
eternaliter puniret vel affligeret sine eius
peccato, vel pure annihilaret, nullam
iniusticiam vel crudelitatem ei faceret [S I
12 J].

. . . aliquis potest fieri de peccatore non
peccator per solam liberam Dei acceptationem
[S IV 1 R; see also S I 9 J, and S I 9 M].

5. Also, there is no essential connection between grace and merit, or grace and eternal life, on the one hand, and between guilt and punishment, or guilt and eternal punishment, on the other. These relationships belong to the order God has established. By his absolute power God can infuse grace and forgive guilt and still leave an obligation to eternal punishment. He can punish eternally someone who has not offended Him. And all this without injustice.

> For, absolutely speaking, God could, without injustice, infuse grace and forgive guilt while the obligation to eternal punishment lasts, as He could punish someone eternally without demerit [in that person].

> Even if God were to punish or afflict a creature eternally without it having sinned, or were simply to annihilate it, He would do no injustice or cruelty to it.

6. God can change a sinner to a non-sinner with no change in the person, simply by freely accepting him.

> By God's free acceptance alone, someone who is a sinner can become not a sinner.

. . . nullam contradictionem implicat quod
Deus ordinaret talem legem quod quicumque
decederet sine caritate vel gratia, tali lege
stante, esset amicus Dei dignus vita eterna .
. . [S I 9 J].

Ergo ei cui dedit caritatem vel gratiam
potest non dare vitam eternam [S I 9 K].

. . . de lege ordinata non est possibile
creaturam rationalem diligere Deum meritorie
sine habitu infuso caritatis vel gratie , . .
. de potentia absoluta est possibile . . . [S
I 9 K; see also S I 9 O].

7. It is not a contradiction for God to declare as a friend, and reward with eternal life, someone dying without charity or grace.

   It implies no contradiction for God to ordain such a law that, such a law being in force, whoever died without charity or grace would be a friend of God, worthy of eternal life.

8. God can refuse eternal life to a person dying in the state of grace.

   Therefore He can refuse eternal life to a person to whom He gave charity or grace.

9. By God's absolute power it is possible for someone to love God without grace and charity.

   By the ordained law it is not possible for a rational creature to love God meritoriously without an infused habit of charity or grace. By [God's] absolute power, it is possible.

10. God can reward and punish whomever He wishes, with no respect to his state or his deeds.

. . . aliquis non dignus vita eterna potest fieri dignus ea de potentia absoluta absque aliqua mutatione in ipso aut in quolibet alio facta propter solam transitionem temporis existentis vel possibilis. Patet quia, sicut rex posset statuere inventos in camera die lune debere puniri et inventos die martis debere premiari, sic nulla est contradictio quod Deus statueret existentes sub A mensura esse habituros beatitudinem et non ante vel post . . . [S I 9 M].

Et ideo est maior vel minor caritas vel gratia secundum quod magis vel minus acceptatur a voluntate divina, id est, ad maiorem vel minorem beatitudinem. Absolute

By [God's] absolute power someone not worthy of eternal life can be made worthy of it without any change being made in him or in anything else, simply because of the passing of real or possible time. This is obvious because, as a king could decree that those found in a room on Monday should be punished, and those found on Tuesday should be rewarded, so there is no contradiction in God decreeing that those existing at time A will have beatitude, and not those before or after.

As we have seen, this is close to what God does anyway. But, by His ordinary power, He provides merits for those He predestines, and demerits for those He reprobates. By His absolute power He can dispense with these merits and demerits.

11. God also ordinarily accepts a greater grace or charity as deserving of a greater beatitude, but He can reward a lesser grace or charity with greater beatitude. And, Peter adds, a person can imagine all sorts of possibilities in these matters if he is clever.

And therefore there is a greater or lesser charity or grace according as it is more or less accepted by the divine will, that is, for a greater or a lesser beatitude. Absolutely, however, the one with the lesser

autem staret quod minor in gradu magis
acceptaretur, et sic maior qualitas esset
minor caritas, et minor qualitas esset maior
caritas. Et ex istis patet via subtilibus ad
imaginandum multa in hac materia [S I 9 DD].

. . . vel loquimur de potentia absoluta, et
sic dico quod in illo casu . . . Deus . . .
potest illud adulterium non deacceptare, et
absolvere ut non sit peccatum . . . [S IV 4
CC].

degree could be more accepted, and thus a greater amount of this quality would be a lesser charity, and a lesser amount of this quality would be a greater charity. And from these considerations a way is open to those who are clever to imagine many things in this matter.

One of these possibilities is that God might not consider adultery sinful.

Or we speak of absolute power, and thus I say that in that case God can cease rejecting adultery, and stop it being a sin.

Summing up Peter's teaching concerning the supernatural order, we see that:

(1) Peter contradicts himself by holding that God knows infallibly, and yet does not know infallibly, future contingent events.

(2) God cannot reveal infallibly a future contingent event, even to Christ or the Blessed.

(3) The Christian faith can contain errors.

(4) God can deceive, by His absolute power.

(5) Human beings are not free.

(6) There are no necessary relationships amongst
    possessing the Holy Spirit, possessing grace and
    charity, possessing faith and hope, being a friend
    of God, meriting or possessing eternal life; nor
    among not possessing the Holy Spirit, not
    possessing grace and charity, not being a friend of
    God, having demerit, or suffering eternal
    punishment; nor amongst any member of the first
    group and any member of the second.

    Many fourteenth century writers taught that
God can deceive [16, pp. 521-524; 28, pp. 65-66] and
held other doctrines identical or similar to Peter's
[28, pp. 50-54].

. . . concessa contingentia respectu
futurorum . . . non potest convinci per
rationes in lumine naturali quin etiam
concedenda sit huiusmodi contingentia
respectu preteritorum [S I 11 H].

. . . hec est possibilis: quod fuit
contingenter non fuit contingenter [S I 11
H].

ALL ORDERS

We have seen that Peter has rendered the physical, the moral, and the supernatural orders contingent to a great extent. We shall now see that each of them is rendered even more contingent because, for Peter, God can undo the past. This means that at each moment whatever God has decreed by His ordained power can be undone so that it never happened. All contingent truths about creatures, at any moment, can cease to be true.

For Peter, the past not only was contingent before it came to be but remains always contingent. No philosophical reason can be found against this.

Granted that there is contingency with respect to matters of the future, it cannot be proven by arguments in the natural light that a contingency of this kind should not be granted also with respect to things that are past.

This is possible: What existed contingently did not exist contingently.

Peter gives four arguments for his position.

. . . si Deus non posset velle modo mundum
non fuisse, igitur esset mutata eius
potentia. Et si Deus, respectu huius quod
est velle mundum non fuisse, habuit aliquando
libertatem contradictionis et nunc non habet,
eius libertas videtur esse mutata quia habuit
prius potentiam et libertatem ad hoc et nunc
non haberet [S I 11 H].

. . . mundum non fuisse aliquando fuit
obiectum divine voluntatis; sed nec ex parte
voluntatis divine, cum sit omnipotens, nec ex
parte obiecti, cum sit eodem modo se habens
nunc et prius, non est defectus quare nunc
non posset esse obiectum divine voluntatis
sicut prius [S I 11 H].

1. If God cannot now will that the world not have been, His power is less than it was. Previously He had the power to will it to be or not to be. If He loses this power after creating the world, He is now less than omnipotent, which cannot be.

    If God could not now will that the world had not been, then His power would have been changed. And if God, as regards willing the world not to have been, at one time had freedom of contradiction and does not have it now, His freedom seems to have been changed because He earlier had the power and the freedom for this and now would not have it.

2. At one time the non-existence of the world was the possible object of the divine will. And the object is just as it was. And the divine will is just as it was, omnipotent.

    At one time it was an object of the divine will that there was not a world. But nothing is lacking why it could not be the object of the divine will now as before, neither on the part of the divine will, since it is omnipotent, nor on the part of the object, since it is just the same now as it was before.

163

. . . quero que sit causa huius necessitatis,
scilicet quare voluntas divina necessitatur
ad volendum mundum fuisse, nec potest velle
mundum non fuisse. Et constat quod non
potest assignari causa nisi obiecti
existentia. Ergo res extra, vel preteritio
rei, necessitaret voluntatem Dei, quod est
absurdum . . . [S I 11 H].

. . . adventus rei non necessitat voluntatem
nostram. Ergo nec per consequens voluntatem
divinam. Antecedens patet quia possumus de
re que fuit velle ipsam non fuisse, sicut
patet de penitente [S I 11 H].

3. God's will cannot be necessitated by any creature.
    So the world cannot necessitate the divine will to
    leave the past as it was. (God is obviously always
    able to annihilate the world; what we are speaking
    of here is the world, which is, never having been.)

    I ask what is the cause of this necessity,
    namely, why the divine will is necessitated
    to will that the world existed and cannot
    will that the world not have existed. And it
    is evident that no reason can be assigned
    except the existence of the object.
    Therefore the external thing, or the pastness
    of the thing, would necessitate the divine
    will, which is absurd.

4. Even we can will that the past not have existed, as
    when we would like not to have sinned. If we can
    do this, so can God. And, since His will is
    supremely efficacious, it would bring this about.

    The coming of a thing does not necessitate
    our will. Therefore, as a consequence, not
    the divine will either. The antecedent is
    clear because, concerning a thing which was,
    we can will that it not have been, as is
    clear in the case of a penitent.

    However, if there is no philosophical
demonstration against the possibility of the world not

. . . non est nobis evidens nec naturaliter
demonstrabile quod aliquod futurum potest non
fore. Patet quia in naturali lumine ita
faciliter, vel non magis difficulter,
sustineretur quod preteritum potest non
fuisse sicut quod futurum potest non fore . .
. . Ergo, si primum non est evidens . . .
sequitur quod nec secundum, sed solum
tenendum est fide [S I 11 H].

. . . Deus non posset facere aliquid non
fuisse, et hoc positive aliquid faciendo, sed
negative non producendo ipsum in preterito.
Hoc est quia potest ipsum non produxisse [S I
11 J].

having been, neither is there one for it. This possibility is justified by faith alone. The human mind can hardly imagine the future not being, or the past not having been. Yet both future and past are contingent.

It is not evident to us, nor naturally demonstrable, that some future thing is able not to be. This is evident because, in the natural light, it would be equally easy or difficult to sustain that the past can not have been and that the future is able not to be. Therefore, if the first is not evident, it follows that the second is not either, but must be held by faith alone.

An objection is offered that God cannot undo the past because it is now non-existent, and there is nothing for God to act on. But Peter answers that the future is also non-existent but God's causality determines it. And, besides, God doesn't act on the past. He simply now exercises the option, initially open to Him, of not producing the world.

God could make something not have been, not positively by doing something, but negatively by not producing it in the past. This is because He has the power to have not produced it.

. . . posset tamen illud facere nigrum sine
mutatione quia posset facere illud numquam
fuisse album et semper fuisse nigrum [S I 11
J].

. . . intelligitur de potentia ordinata [S I
11 J].

. . . per experientiam evidenter et clare
cognoscimus aliquod preteritum fuisse . . .
sed . . . non sic clare cognoscimus aliquid

A second objection is that God would have to be able to do things such as make a white object black if he were able to undo the past, and do this without any change. But this is impossible. Peter answers that God would not have to make a white object black, but rather make a black object be present _instead_ _of_ a white one, and that He could do this without any change.

> He could however make that thing black without any change because He could make it never have been white, and always have been black.

A final objection poses the problem of whether God could make a non-virgin a virgin by undoing the past. Peter answers that certainly He could, but only by His absolute power.

> This is understood of ordained power.

Peter says that we say the future cannot be because we haven't experienced it yet, but we find it hard to say the past can not be because we _have_ experienced it.

> We know evidently and clearly by experience that something has been in the past, but we do not know so clearly that something will be

futurum fore. Ideo facilius imaginamur illud posse non fore quam illud posse non fuisse . . . [S I 11 J].

Similiter oportet concedere ad salvandam contingentiam futurorum quod Deus aliquid ab eterno scivit et voluit quod potest numquam scivisse aut voluisse . . . [S I 11 H].

. . . de nullo intellectu qui iudicavit Antichristum vel iudicium fore concedendum est quod post hoc non iudicasse nisi de illo de quo ista consequentia est bona: Iste intellectus sic iudicavit; ergo sic erit. Sed de solo intellectu divino et nullo alio ista consequentia est bona . . . [S III principium J; see also S I 12 KK].

in the future. Therefore we more easily
imagine it to be able not to be in the future
than it to be able not to have been.

Peter uses this doctrine of the contingency
of the past in order to solve the problem of God's
knowledge of future contingents. Since they are truly
contingent, what God eternally knew and willed
concerning them may not be realized. Now, if God's
knowledge cannot be false, we will have to say that He
could never have known and willed what He eternally
knew and willed.

Similarly we have to grant, in order to save
the contingency of future things, that God
knew and willed something from eternity which
He can never have known or willed.

This would be true only of God, of course, since only
His knowledge is guaranteed to be infallible. It would
not apply to a creature.

Concerning no intellect which judged that
there would be an Antichrist or a Judgment
must it be granted that, after this, it did
not judge this, except concerning the
intellect of which this argumentation is
sound: "This intellect judged thus; therefore
it will be thus." But this argumentation is
sound of the divine intellect alone and no
other.

171

. . . dico quod, si ponatur quod preteritum
non potest non fuisse, nulla predictarum
viarum est sufficiens, nec est alia dabilis,
quin oporteat dicere quod . . . Deus potest
falsum dicere et decipere . . . ita quod
oportet dicere vel quod preteritum potest non
fuisse vel quod Deus falsum potest dixisse.
Nec est dare medium . . . [S I 12 GG].

The only way in which this is possible for Peter, without violating the first principle, is for the past to be undone. Meller [35, p. 236] says that Peter thinks the first principle can be violated in this case. Perhaps Peter at some point in his work did think this, but he nowhere explicitly says so. And he does have another way out, since he teaches that the past can be undone. According to Peter, only this teaching can prevent having to say that God can deceive. There is no other way.

> I say that, if it is posited that the past
> can have not existed, none of the aforesaid
> positions is sufficient, nor is there another
> available, to prevent us having to say that
> God can say what is false and deceive; so
> that it is necessary to say either that the
> past can have not existed or that God can
> have spoken what is false. Nor is there a
> middle position.

If God has made an eternal judgment about a contingent event, and the event does not correspond to it, God can wipe out the uncooperative event and start the world over, hoping that this time things will work out better.

Peter does not make clear whether God would have to undo the whole of the past or only a certain part of it.

This doctrine of the contingency of the past is one of the most sceptical doctrines imaginable. To think that creation could be undone, that all historical "truths" could become false, that immortal souls enjoying the Beatific Vision could cease to be, that the Son of God could not have become man! Only necessary truths would remain. The natural sciences, history, revelation; all would be gone. We thus see that for Peter the physical order, the moral order, and the supernatural order, are highly contingent in their nature but, in addition, are doubly contingent because the physical and human beings which they tell us about could, in whole or in part, never have been.

Other fourteenth-century writers besides Peter taught that the past is contingent and can be undone. For example, this was taught by Thomas Bradwardine (before 1344), Gregory of Rimini (by 1345), and Nicholas Aston (c. 1350) [4; 38, p. 7; 21].

CONCLUSION

Oberman has shown [42] that the influence of William of Ockham was widespread in the two centuries following Ockham, and that it manifested itself in different ways, or to different degrees. He has also rightly pointed out that the key doctrine of the Nominalism issuing from Ockham was an over-riding concern with, and a certain interpretation of, God's absolute power. He further claims that there were four chief results of this: (1) a heightened awareness of God's sovereignty, (2) a heightened awareness of God's immediacy, (3) a greater emphasis on man's autonomy and freedom, (4) scepticism. As concerns the first three of these doctrines, the evidence he adduces for his claim is insufficient to establish it. One would find as much insistence on God's sovereignty and immediacy, and man's autonomy and freedom, in the teaching of St. Thomas Aquinas, for example. But Oberman is certainly correct concerning scepticism.

Some of the authors who have written about Peter of Ailly's theory of knowledge have denied the charge of scepticism levelled against it. Desharnais, for example [9, p. 304], says that "Ailly's epistemology agrees with the general doctrine of the major schoolmen." But Desharnais is wrong. The major schoolmen do not agree with one another, and it would be difficult to say what general epistemological

doctrine they held. Peter of Ailly agrees with William of Ockham in fundamental epistemology, taking its principles much further than Ockham, and into scepticism. But he certainly does not agree with St. Thomas Aquinas or Duns Scotus.

De Gandillac also tries to refute the charge of scepticism. He claims that the doubts expressed in Peter's Sentences are simply methodological (8, pp. 44-45); that when Peter speaks of probability he really means a kind of certainty (p. 46); and that, when it is said that God's absolute power can lead us to be mistaken about the first principle, the error in question is a purely verbal one (p. 54). This sanguine view is not universal, however.

Manser [31] is well aware of Peter's tendency to scepticism concerning physical causality and concerning moral matters, but doesn't connect it to the question of divine omnipotence. He teaches rather that it is the result of Peter's nominalist doctrine of universals. Now, though one can show that Peter's doctrine of God's absolute power and his doctrine of universals have a common source, the truth is that his scepticism comes from his teaching concerning God's absolute power.

The study of Peter's whole theory of knowledge which faces up best to the charge of scepticism is Meller's [35]. But Meller seems satisfied with very little. He absolves Peter from the charge of complete scepticism because for Peter the first principle is always true [p. 109]. Meller is aware that Peter's doctrine of evidence is like that of

John of Mirecourt [p. 99] and that his doctrine of causality is like that of Nicholas of Autrecourt [p. 110]; yet he seems to be unaware of Peter's thoroughgoing implicit scepticism. Though he mentions Peter's doctrine concerning the absolute power of God, he does not take its consequences seriously. Perhaps, like Peter, he did not realize that there is no guarantee that it might not be exercised at any time.

Indeed, most authors who have written about Peter have had the same conviction. They have thought that, though God's use of His absolute power would nullify in whole or in part the created physical, moral, or supernatural order, as a matter of fact one could be sure that God would never use it. This is held by Courtenay [3, p. 95, n. 4] when writing about Peter; and McDonnell [34, p. 392] and Oberman [43, p. 57] make the same point about Nominalists in general. Lindbeck is so convinced on this point that he thinks the introduction of a consideration of God's absolute power in Peter's doctrine of sensation "does not indicate the slightest trace of scepticism" [30, p. 56].

Oakley is very much aware of the tenuous grasp of the human mind on truth, according to Peter. Though he writes almost entirely of the moral order [41], his judgment is sound:

. . . created titles, created laws, created causes--all of these are dissolved into nothingness in the blaze of the divine omnipotence [41, p. 195].

181

Let us consider, then, to what extent Peter can be called a sceptic.

If we set aside for the moment the question whether God might ever exercise his absolute power, and limit ourselves to the ordained order, Peter teaches that we can be sure, with absolute evidence, of:

1. The first principle.

2. All conclusions following from it, such as the science of mathematics.

3. Some contingent truths, such as "I exist," "I am thinking."

He also teaches that we can be sure, with conditional evidence, of:

1. The existence and nature of the physical world.

2. Only one substance in itself, our own.

3. The causes of the things we see happening.

4. The physical sciences.

5. The moral order indicated by our conscience and by divine revelation, though of this order the only non-arbitrary truth is that we must obey God not because of what He has commanded but simply because He has commanded.

6. The supernatural order revealed by God.

If we were to agree that God will never use his absolute power, we might think that Peter is not exceedingly sceptical, perhaps faulting him with relegating most of our knowledge to a second-class (though still reliable) level, denying our ability to know most substances, making the moral order to a great extent arbitrary, and saying that philosophy, without faith, would lead us to think that the human soul is probably not immortal and that the existence and nature of God can be discovered only with probability.

We might even point out that, since the difference between absolute and conditional evidence for Peter involves God's ability to exercise His absolute power, all evidence is absolute evidence if indeed God will never use this power.

However, if God can use His absolute power, the physical, moral, and supernatural orders, all that God has ordained, hang by a thread from the divine will, the divine wisdom and goodness being unable to prevent the thread being severed at any moment. All we could be sure of would be:

(1) The first principle.

(2) Conclusions following from it, such as the science of mathematics.

(3) The existence of God, and His attributes such as simplicity, eternity, omnipotence, intelligence, or triune nature. And this only through faith.

185

(4) Some contingent truths, such as "I am," "I am thinking."

(5) We are bound to obey God, if He commands us.

The most important question, then, is whether, in Peter's theory of knowledge, God can use His absolute power once He has established the present order of things. There are really two questions involved here, the less important being whether Peter thought God can use His absolute power, the more important being whether, given Peter's principles, God can use His absolute power.

The answer to the first question is that Peter may have thought that God would never use His absolute power, but that, if he thought this, he should never have written the book he wrote. In other words, he is filled with contradictions.

In favour of the interpretation that Peter thought God will not use His absolute power are two groups of texts, quite few in number. The first group deals with the objects of sensation, with causality, and with the physical sciences. Peter says that, though we cannot be perfectly sure that objects we sense really exist, it is unreasonable to doubt that they do. If we were to doubt whether God were exercising His absolute power, we would be in a deplorable state. We would not know whether what looked like an ass might really be God. We would not know whether a particular event had such-and-such a cause, and so all natural sciences would be untrustworthy. We would be overwhelmed by questions and absurdities.

Unde, quamvis talis apparentia possit esse, ipsis obiectis non existentibus per potentiam Dei absolutam, tamen propter hoc non habemus rationabiliter dubitare. Nam ex hoc multa inconvenientia et absurda sequerentur.

. . . possemus rationabiliter dubitare quod aliqua substantia, alia a natura nostra, divina esset, quia Deus posset conservare omnia accidentia huiusmodi, substantiis corruptis seu destructis, ut in sacramento altaris.

. . . non posset sufficienter inferri, ex una re, alia; nec ex causa posset concludi effectus, nec econtra; et sic perirent omnes demonstrationes naturales.

. . . haberemus rationabiliter dubitare, demonstrata quacumque creatura, an illa esset Deus, an illa esset adoranda, et sic an Deus esset asinus, an asinus [esset] adorandus. Nam quamlibet talem posset Deus assumere, etc. [S I 1 F].

Hence, although there can be such an appearance, with its objects not existing because of God's absolute power, still this does not force our reason to doubt [its veracity], because many incongruities and absurdities would follow from this.

We could rationally doubt whether some substance, other than our own nature, might be divine, because God could conserve all the accidents of this kind after their substances were corrupted or destroyed, as in the Sacrament of the Altar.

From one thing there would not be sufficient reason for another to be inferred. Nor could an effect be concluded from a cause, nor vice versa. And thus all natural demonstrations would perish.

If any creature were pointed out, our reason would have to doubt whether it were God, whether it should be adored, and thus whether God were an ass, whether an ass should be adored. For God could assume any of these.

If Peter were at Paris, he could be at Rome at the same time. God could make him show up as a thousand men and defeat as many men in battle. But Peter doesn't have

. . . ego existens Parisius simul tempore possum esse Rome. Non tamen habeo dubitare me esse Rome quia, licet Deus possit hoc facere et non sit mihi evidens evidentia summa, sive evidentia simpliciter absoluta, utrum sic faciat, tamen debeo credere quod non facit. Nam hoc non possit facere sine miraculo, et ego debeo credere quod non facit miraculum nisi appareat probabiliter de opposito.

. . . de potentia Dei ego possum esse ubique et apparere mille homines et vincere in bello mille homines vel omnes. Et multa similia sequuntur, sed non habeo de istis dubitare sic esse propter illa que iam dixi [S IV 5 DD].

Consequentia tenet quia ista communis regula, quod agente approximato passivo [the text has to doubt whether he might be at Rome, or fighting an army all by himself, unless there is some reason for thinking that God is working a miracle.

Existing in Paris, I can be in Rome at the same time. However, I do not have to doubt about whether I am in Rome because, although God could bring this about, and it is not evident to me with the highest evidence, or simply absolute evidence, whether He is doing it, still I ought to believe that He is not doing it. For He could not do this without a miracle, and I ought to believe that He doesn't perform a miracle unless it appears that this is probably not the case.

By God's power I can be everywhere, and can seem to be a thousand men, and conquer a thousand men, or everyone, in battle. And many things like this follow, but I do not have to doubt about whether these are really true, for the reasons I have already given.

The second group of texts states Peter's general principle that one should assume that God is not using His absolute power unless the contrary is indicated by Scripture, reason, or experience.

The argumentation holds because this common rule (that action follows when the agent is

passo] disposito sequitur actio, non est
neganda nisi obviet sibi auctoritas scripture
. . . vel ratio . . . vel experientia . . .
[S IV 5 NN].

. . . in fide Christi numquam neganda est
apparentia sensus naturaliter bene dispositi
nisi ubi expressa auctoritas vel efficax ratio
sumpta ex his que sunt fidei ad hoc cogit [S
IV 1 N].

> brought near to the properly disposed
> patient) must not be denied unless scriptural
> authority, or reason, or experience,
> indicates otherwise.

> In the faith of Christ, an appearance to a
> sense naturally and properly disposed should
> never be denied unless where an express
> authority, or an efficacious reason taken
> from matters of faith, necessitates it.

It should be pointed out that Peter is somewhat exceptional in giving a reason to think God might not use His absolute power. John Went, for example, has some of the wildest imaginable possibilities of the use of God's absolute power and never hints that God might not use this power [24]. And a questio in the notebook of Stephen Patrington, at Oxford about the same time Peter was writing his Sentences at Paris, tries to give a reason but the writer realizes that the reason is not very strong [22]. How is one to interpret these texts of Peter? One might say that they express his conviction that God will not use His absolute power, since He has established the natural and supernatural orders, which provide us with Scripture, reason, and experience.

We are prepared to accept this as a possible interpretation of what Peter would have said, had we been able to ask him. But it is important to point out that nearly everything in Peter's Sentences runs counter to this interpretation. Peter is obsessed with

. . . nihil aliud a Deo est aut esse potest,
saltem secundum legem statutam pro nunc,
ordinate fruitionis obiectum [S IV 1 N].

the notion of God's absolute power. Now, if he really thought that God will never use this power, why would he refer to it at every turn? Why would he spend his time, in his discussion of God's love, in explaining that God can command us to hate Him; in his discussion of eternal life, in explaining that God can annihilate or damn the Blessed; in his discussion of the Incarnation, in wondering whether Christ could have assumed the humanity of Mary and thus have been His own mother [S III 1 N]? Peter's practice belies a mild interpretation of his doctrine.

Besides, since Peter clearly teaches that God can be mistaken concerning future contingents, and that God's undoing of the past is the only way to prevent God actually making a mistake, Peter must think that God might actually use His absolute power.

Moreover, a text of Peter seems to indicate that he thinks God can use His absolute power. Peter says that only God can be the proper object of the human will according to the dispensation put in place for now.

> Nothing other than God is or can be, at least
> according to the law presently established,
> the object of proper enjoyment.

Also, Peter defends his predecessor at the University of Paris, Nicholas of Autrecourt, whose statements were censured by the Roman Curia, in Avignon, in 1346. Many of Peter's doctrines resemble

Multa fuerunt condemnata contra eum [Nicholas of Autrecourt] causa invidie, quae tamen postea in scholis publice sunt concessa [48, f. 15v].

Nicholas's. In particular, Nicholas held that we cannot be sure that an apparent secondary cause is a real cause, because God could be using His absolute power to dispense with a secondary cause [19, p. 37]. And Nicholas nowhere says that God is prevented by the present dispensation from exercising his absolute power. And Peter claims that Nicholas's statements were condemned not because they were false but out of envy:

> Because of envy, many things were condemned vis-à-vis Nicholas of Autrecourt which were however publicly granted later in the schools.

Peter thus seems to indicate that he thinks God can exercise His absolute power.

We may thus conclude that, if Peter was of the opinion that God will never use His absolute power, his chief concern in the Sentences is an unnecessary one; his doctrine implicitly contradicts this opinion; and one of his texts, and his defense of Nicholas, seem to do so as well.

The more important question remains, however: given Peter's principles, can one be sure God will not use His absolute power? Quite a few contemporary historians of the fourteenth century, writing about Peter or other Nominalists, claim that the answer is yes. We have seen that this is true of Courtenay, McDonnell, Oberman, and Lindbeck.

Courtenay gives two reasons for his position.
The first is that God's use of His absolute power would
be unjust once He established the present order of
things. Speaking of Nominalists in general, he says:

> This does not mean, however, that for the
> Nominalists God's action is arbitrary or
> likely to be reversed . . . . God always acts
> wisely . . . because he possesses an inward
> sense of justice . . . [3, p. 117].

Courtenay's position is that God has made a two-fold
covenant with the human race: that He will not use His
absolute power in the natural order or in the
supernatural order [3, p. 117].

This, of course, is a faulty position. For
Peter, God is not bound by any criterion of justice
except that whatever God does is just. And, indeed,
how could one ever appeal to the justice of a God who
can damn for eternity a person who loves Him and reward
with eternal bliss one who hates him? And, assuming
for the moment that God has made a covenant to preserve
the present dispensation, why should He be trusted
since, according to Peter, He can deceive?

Peter of Ailly does not make the mistake of
appealing to divine justice other than in the present
order of things. For him, God's power is not limited
by justice. Justice is what God has set down as such
in the natural or supernatural orders; His power is
above this "justice."

. . . quedam Deus potest de potentia que non potest de iustitia. Illud enim dicitur non posse de iustitia quod obviat ordinationi sue voluntatis vel veritati sue legis,quarum utraque est regula iustitia. Sed illud dicitur posse de potentia absoluta quod absolute et simpliciter potest quamvis oppositum ordinaverit vel revelaverit [S I 13 C].

God can do by His power some things which He cannot do by His justice. For He is said not to be able to do by His justice what is opposed to the ordination of His will, or the truth of His law, each of which is a rule of justice. But He is said to be able to do by absolute power what He can do absolutely and simply, although He has ordained or revealed the opposite of this.

Courtenay's second reason for saying that God will not use His absolute power is that its use is ruled out because God is consistent in His actions. Courtenay, referring to Peter and to others, writes:

Since God has obliged himself to work in particular ways and, being omniscient and consistent, will not deviate from the divine plan for creation, the choices initially open to God are no longer real possibilities once the divine plan is established [7, p. 249].

No one that I have examined on the question of God's power to make a past thing never have been ever envisaged God's wishing to change the past. That is excluded from the realm of real possibility because of the ordained order and the consistency of divine action [4, v. 40, p. 166].

Now, Peter nowhere teaches that consistency is _per se_ a divine attribute. And, indeed, if it is not founded on wisdom and justice, why would it be seen even as desirable?

What happens in many cases is that an attempt to exalt divine power results in a reduction of it. If one says that God can cause his rational creatures to deny the first principle, one takes away His power to give them evident knowledge. If one says that God can deceive us, one takes away His power to have us trust unreservedly in His word. If one says that God could have established an almost totally different moral order, one takes away His power to have us accept without question the one He has established. If one says that God can act without regard to His wisdom or goodness, one takes away His power to have us accept His actions as wise or good. If one says that future contingents are so utterly in God's power that even He cannot know them, one takes away His power to know future contingents or to guarantee the Blessed their eternal happiness. And, if one says that, before God, the present order of things is utterly contingent, one takes away His power to guarantee this order. We look in vain for necessity in a thoroughly contingent universe. Once God's absolute power is unleashed, there is no recapturing it. If one wishes to hold that God _will_ _not_ arbitrarily undo the present dispensation, he will have to say that God _cannot_ undo it. He will have to restrict God's power to establishing an arbitrarily-chosen universe so that, once such a universe is established, there is no more absolute power. But what proponent of the doctrine of divine absolute power openly speaks in this manner? And,

203

. . . in Deo, inter voluntatem et intellectum
. . . nulla est omnino distinctio [S II
principium M].

. . . voluntas divina et divinus intellectus
seu ratio sunt omnibus modis idem tam
formaliter quam realiter, nec distinguunter
inter se aliqualiter [S II principium F].

indeed, how could he convincingly do so? The modern-day proponents of this doctrine want it both ways. They want many things to be possible by God's absolute power and also to be impossible. But, having initially refused divine wisdom and goodness the ability to restrict God's power, they cannot later successfully call upon divine "justice" and consistency to do so. After the establishment of the natural and supernatural orders, "God's absolute power" is either a frightening ever-present threat or a dead concept; there is no middle path.

Another approach to the defense of the doctrine of divine absolute power is taken by some of the writers named. They say God's actions cannot be arbitrary because, according to Peter in particular, and Nominalists in general, the divine intellect and will are identical [3, p. 117; 43, p. 61; 9, p. 304].

Now, it is true that, for Peter, the divine intellect and will are absolutely identical, since God is simple.

> In God there is absolutely no distinction between will and intellect.

> The divine will and the divine intellect or reason are the same in every way, both formally and really, nor are they distinguished from one another in any way.

These _are_ one another.

. . . voluntas divina est intellectus divinus, et econtra [S II principium F].

. . . ita proprie et de virtute sermonis verum est quod voluntas divina est ratio summa sicut quod intellectus divinus est ratio summa . . . [S II principium H].

. . . falsum est quod . . . veritas [non est] obiectum voluntatis divine . . . [S II principium H].

. . . cum voluntas divina sit veritas summa [S I principium E; see also S II principium G].

The divine will is the divine intellect, and vice versa.

It is as true to say that the divine will is the highest reason as it is to say that the divine intellect is.

Thus, properly and as the words indicate, it is true that the divine will is the highest reason just as the divine intellect is the highest reason.

Indeed, truth is the object of the divine will.

It is false that truth is not the object of the divine will.

. . . since the divine will is the highest truth.

This identity of the divine intellect and will is so great that there is not even a mental distinction between them. If two things are really distinct, they cannot be mentally the same, and two things mentally distinct cannot be really the same. Thus two things really the same cannot be mentally distinct.

. . . sicut deitas et divinus intellectus seu
voluntas non distinguuntur realiter inter se,
sic nec proprie loquendo distinguuntur
ratione [S I 6 L].

. . . unde, sicut distincta realiter non sunt
idem secundum rationem, sic nec eadem
realiter sunt distincta secundum rationem [S
I 6 L].

. . . sicut divina voluntas nullam habet
rationem propter quam determinetur ut velit,
sic divinus intellectus propter divine
voluntatis determinationem non assentit quod
Antichristus erit [S IV principium E].

As deity and the divine intellect or will are
not really distinguished from one another, so
neither are they distinguished mentally,
properly speaking.

Hence, as things which are really distinct
are not the same mentally, so neither are
things really the same distinct mentally.

One might easily think that this doctrine would lead to
the conclusion that the divine power is so impregnated
by the divine intellect that whatever God does is wise,
that God is unable to have any power to act in an
arbitrary fashion. Yet other texts of Peter prevent us
from coming to this conclusion. He interprets the
identity of the divine intellect and will as ruling out
interaction between them.

As the divine will has no reason for
determining itself to will, so the divine
intellect's assent that Antichrist will come
is not on account of a determination of the
divine will.

Peter makes this clear in the relationship between
divine power and divine mercy. These are thoroughly
identical. This does not mean, however, that every use
of divine power will be merciful. On the contrary,
God's absolute power can act independently of His
mercy.

Unde etiam, cum potentia Dei et eius misericordia penitus idem sint, si aliquid potest de potentia inquantum potentia, absolute potest illud, non obstante misericordia [S I 12 AA].

Et si hoc non repugnet potentie Dei inquantum potentia, repugnat tamen potentie inquantum est summa benignitas et summa misericordia [S I 12 AA].

Sed hec opinio sufficit quia eque faciliter defenderetur error ille philosophorum quorundam, scilicet quod quidquid Deus agit

Hence also, since the power of God and His
mercy are utterly the same, if He can do
something by His power considered as power,
He can do it absolutely speaking, without
regard to His mercy.

The doctrine of the identity of divine power
and mercy is thus for Peter not a means of guaranteeing
the mercifulness of God's power but a way of allowing
absolute power to act without being tempered by mercy.

This doctrine is given in response to the
argument that God could not annihilate the Blessed
because such an act would be opposed to His mercy.

And if this is not opposed to God's power as
power, it is nevertheless opposed to this
power inasmuch as it is the highest kindness
and highest mercy.

Peter thinks that to deny to God the real power of
acting against His mercy would be an unjustifiable
restraint on His power. It would be a removal of
divine freedom in relationship to creatures, and like
the position of certain philosophers who said God is
necessitated.

But this opinion is sufficient because that
error of certain philosophers (namely, that
whatever God does outside Himself He does by

ad extra agit nature necessitate . . . [S I
12 AA].

a necessity of nature) could be defended equally easily.

Peter is therefore not speaking of an absolute power of God which can not be exercised unless restrained by the divine intellect; he is speaking of a _real_ power, limited only by the first principle.

A further consideration leading to the conclusion that God's absolute power is not bound by what He has done is that by this power, according to Peter, He can undo the past, make it so that it has never been. Now, if He can do this He cannot be restricted by what is or what has been. All of it can be rendered non-present and non-past. There is no obstacle whatever to God's absolute power. No established order can bind His justice or consistency.

We thus see that, though Peter's modern-day defenders think that his doctrine of divine absolute power does not lead to scepticism, in fact it does so. These persons, like most sceptics, strain out the gnat and swallow the camel. They accept the doctrine that the divine absolute power can act without restraint from the divine wisdom and goodness, and yet teach that this power is inoperative once God has created a universe. They give creation a restraining power the divine nature lacks.

SELECTIVE BIBLIOGRAPHY

1. J. L. Bender, Nicholas Aston: A Study in Oxford Thought after the Black Death. Xerox University Microfilms, Ann Arbor, 1979.

2. Chartularium Universitatis Parisiensis, tome II, sect. 1 (Paris, 1891).

3. W. J. Courtenay, "Covenant and Causality in Pierre d'Ailly," Speculum, XLVI (1971) 94-119.

4. W. J. Courtenay, "John of Mirecourt and Gregory of Rimini on Whether God Can Undo the Past," Recherches de théologie ancienne et médiévale, 39 (1972) 224-256; 40 (1973) 147-174.

5. W. J. Courtenay, "The Critique on Natural Causality in the Mutakallimum and Nominalism," Harvard Theological Review, 66 (1973) 77-94.

6. W. J. Courtenay, Covenant and Causality in Medieval Thought. London, 1984.

7. W. J. Courtenay, "The Dialectic of Omnipotence in the High and Late Middle Ages," in T. Rudavsky, ed., Divine Omniscience and Omnipotence in Medieval Philosophy (Dordrecht etc., 1985) 243-269.

8. M. P. de Gandillac, "De l'usage et la valeur des arguments probables dans les Questions du Cardinal Pierre d'Ailly sur le 'Livre des Sentences', <u>Archives</u> <u>d'histoire</u> <u>doctrinale</u> <u>et</u> <u>littéraire</u> <u>du</u> <u>moyen âge</u>, 8 (1932-33) 43-91.

9. R. P. Desharnais, "Reassessing Nominalism: A Note on the Epistemology and Metaphysics of Pierre d'Ailly," <u>Franciscan</u> <u>Studies</u>, 34 (1974) 296-305.

10. A. Emmen, "Peter of Ailly (Alliaco)," <u>New</u> <u>Catholic</u> <u>Encyclopedia</u> (Washington, 1967) XI, 208.

11. J.-F. Genest, "Le <u>De</u> <u>futuris</u> <u>contingentibus</u> de Thomas Bradwardine," <u>Recherches</u> <u>Augustiniennes</u>, XIV (1979) 249-336.

12. R. E. Gillespie, <u>Gratia</u> <u>Creata</u> <u>and</u> <u>Acceptatio</u> <u>Divina</u> <u>in</u> <u>the</u> <u>Theology</u> <u>of</u> <u>Robert</u> <u>Holcot</u> <u>O.P.</u> Xerox University Microfilms, Ann Arbor, 1974.

13. P. Glorieux, "Le chancelier Gerson et la réforme de l'enseignement," <u>Mélanges</u> <u>offerts</u> <u>à</u> <u>Etienne</u> <u>Gilson</u> (Toronto, Paris, 1959) 285-298.

14. P. Glorieux, "L'oeuvre littéraire de Pierre d'Ailly. Remarques et précisions," <u>Mélanges</u> <u>de</u> <u>science</u> <u>religieuse</u>,22 (1965) 61-78.

15. P. Glorieux, "Les années d'études de Pierre d'Ailly," <u>Recherches</u> <u>de</u> <u>théologie</u> <u>ancienne</u> <u>et</u> <u>médiévale</u>, XLIV (1977) 127-149.

16. T. Gregory, "La tromperie divine," Studi Medievali, 3ª Serie, XXIII (1982) 517-527.

17. E. Hartmann, "Die sinnliche Wahrnehmung nach Peter d'Ailly," Philosophisches Jahrbuch, XIV (1903) 36-48, 139-148.

18. L. A. Kennedy, The Universal Treatise of Nicholas of Autrecourt. Milwaukee, 1971.

19. L. A. Kennedy, "Philosophical Scepticism in England in the Mid-Fourteenth Century," Vivarium, XXI (1983) 35-57.

20. L. A. Kennedy, "Theology the Handmaiden of Logic," Augustiniana, 33 (1983) 142-163.

21. L. A. Kennedy, "Divine Omnipotence and the Contingency of Creatures, Oxford, 1330-1350 A.D.," The Modern Schoolman, 61 (1983-84).

22. L. A. Kennedy, "Late Fourteenth-century Philosophical Scepticism at Oxford," Vivarium, XXIII (1985).

23. L. A. Kennedy, "A Fourteenth-century Oxford Augustinian on the Existence of God," Augustiniana, 35 (1985).

24. L. A. Kennedy, with M. Romano, "John Went, O.F.M., and Divine Omnipotence," Franciscan Studies, 43 (1983).

25. D. Knowles, "A Characteristic of the Mental Climate of the Fourteenth Century," Mélanges offerts à Etienne Gilson (Toronto, Paris, 1959) 315-325.

26. J. Lappe, "Nicholas von Autrecourt. . . ," Beiträge zur Geschichte der Philosophie des Mittelalters VI, 2 (Munster, 1908) 1*-48*, 1-31.

27. G. Leff, Richard Fitzralph . . . . Manchester, 1963.

28. G. Leff, The Dissolution of the Medieval Outlook. New York, 1976.

29. M. Lieberman, "Peter von Ailly," Lexikon für Theologie und Kirche, 8 (Freiburg, 1963) 300.

30. G. Lindbeck, "Nominalism and the Problem of Meaning as Illustrated by Pierre d'Ailly on Predestination and Justification," Harvard Theological Review, 52 (1959) 43-60.

31. G. M. Manser, "Drei Zweifler am Kausalprinzip im XIV Jahrhundert," Jahrbuck für Philosophie und Spekulative Theologie, XXVII (1912) 291-305, 405-437.

32. A. A. Maurer, "Some Aspects of Fourteenth-century Philosophy," Medievalia et Humanistica, 7 (1976) 175-188.

33. A. A. Maurer, "Ockham on the Possibility of a Better World," Mediaeval Studies 38 (1976) 291-312.

34. K. McDonnell, "Does William of Ockham have a Theory of Natural Law?", Franciscan Studies 34 (1974) 383-392.

35. B. Meller, Studien zur Erkenntnislehre des Peter von Ailly. Freiburg, 1954.

36. K. Michalski, La philosophie au XIVe siècle. Reprint, Frankfurt, 1969.

37. B. Nardi, Soggetto e Oggetto del Conoscere nella Filosofia Antica e Medievale. Rome, 1952.

38. C. G. Normore, "Divine Omniscience, Omnipotence, and Future Contingents: An Overview," in T. Rudavsky, ed., Divine Omniscience and Omnipotence in Medieval Philosophy (Dordrecht etc., 1985) 3-22.

39. F. Oakley, "Medieval Theories of Natural Law: William of Ockham and the Significance of the Voluntarist Tradition," Natural Law Forum, 6 (1961) 65-83.

40. F. Oakley, "Pierre d'Ailly and the Absolute Power of God," The Harvard Theological Review, 56 (1963) 59-73.

41. F. Oakley, The Political Thought of Pierre d'Ailly. New Haven and London, 1964.

42. F. Oakley, "Pierre d'Ailly," in B. A. Gerrish, ed., Reformers in Profile (Philadelphia, 1967) 40-57.

43. H. A. Oberman, "Some Notes on the Theology of Nominalism," Harvard Theological Review, 53 (1960) 47-76.

44. H. A. Oberman, The Harvest of Medieval Theology. Cambridge, Mass., 1963.

45. J. R. O'Donnell, "Nicholas of Autrecourt," Mediaeval Studies, I (1939) 179-280.

46. Peter of Ailly, Quaestiones super libros sententiarum . . . . Strassburg, 1490; Frankfurt, 1968.

47. Peter of Ailly, De Anima. Paris, 1505.

48. Peter of Ailly, Conceptus et Insolubilia. Paris, sine anno.

49. Peter of Ailly, De libertate creaturae rationalis ante et post lapsum, in Jean Gerson, Opera Omnia, ed. L. E. Dupin, I (Antwerp, 1706) 630-641.

50. G. Ritter, Studien zur Spätscholastik. Heidelberg, I, 1921; II, 1922; III, 1927.

51. L. Salembier, Petrus de Alliaco. Lille, 1886.

52. L. Salembier, "Pierre d'Ailly," Dictionnaire de Théologie Catholique, 1 (Paris, 1902) 642-654.

53. L. Salembier, Le cardinal d'Ailly. Besançon, 1909.

54. L. Salembier, "Pierre d'Ailly," _Dictionnaire d'histoire et géographie ecclésiastique_, 1 (Paris, 1912) 1154-65.

55. L. Salembier, _Le cardinal Pierre d'Ailly_. Tourcoing, 1931.

56. P. V. Spade, _Peter of Ailly: Concepts and Insolubles_. Dordrecht etc., 1980.

57. F. Stegmuller, "Die zwei Apologien des Jean de Mirecourt," _Recherches de théologie ancienne et médiévale_, V (1933) 40-78, 192-204.

58. F. Stegmuller, _Repertorium commentariorum in sententias Petri Lombardi_, I (Wurzburg, 1947) nn. 649-651.

59. D.Trapp, "Augustinian Theology of the 14th Century," _Augustiniana_, 6 (1956) 146-274.

60. P. Tschackert, _Peter von Ailli_. Gotha, 1877.

61. William of Ockham, _Super 4 libros Sententiarum_, lib. I (Lyons, 1495; London, 1962).

INDEX

Absolute Power
  and accidents, 71-77
  and causality, 65-67
  and contraries, 67-71
  and deceit, 133-135
  and future contingents, 111-121, 171-173
  and mercy, 209-213
  and omnipotence, 201-205
  and revelation, 121-133
  and scepticism, 1-2, 177-213
  and sensation, 59-65, 73-77
  and sin, 135
  definition, 21-27
  use, 27-29, 181-213
Adam Wodeham, 3
Aristotle, 3, 35
Assent, 7, 11
Avicenna, 3

Boethius, 3, 117

Courtenay, W. J., 23, 27-29, 181, 197-203

De Gandillac, M. P., 179
Desharnais, R. P., 177-179
Duns Scotus, 3, 179